I. *Birmelin and A. Wolter*

The New Parakeet Handbook

Everything about the Purchase, Diet, Diseases,
and Behavior of Parakeets
With a Special Chapter on Raising Parakeets

40 Color Photographs by Outstanding Animal
Photographers and 50 Drawings by Fritz W. Kölher

Translated from the German by Rita and Robert Kimber
American Advisory Editor: Matthew M. Vriends, Ph.D.

BARRON'S

Woodbury, New York/London/Toronto/Sydney

The color photos on the covers show

Front cover: A light green and a sky blue parakeet male.

Inside front cover: Two hand-tame parakeets about eight weeks old.

Inside back cover: Parakeets and cockatiels get along well.

First English language edition published in 1986 by Barron's Educational Series, Inc.

© 1985 by Gräfe and Unzer GmbH, Munich, West Germany

The title of the German book is *Das GU Wellensittich Buch*

All inquiries should be addressed to:
Barron's Educational Series, Inc.
113 Crossways Park Drive
Woodbury, New York 11797

International Standard Book No. 0–8120–2985–2

Library of Congress Catalog Card No. 85–26811

Library of Congress Cataloging-in-Publication Data

Birmelin, I. (Immanuel)
   The new parakeet handbook.

   Translation of: Das GU-Wellensittich-Buch.
   Bibliography: p.
   Includes index.
   1. Budgerigars.   I. Wolter, Annette.   II. Title.
SF473.B8B5713   1986   636.6'864   85–26811
ISBN 0–8120–2985–2

Printed in Hong Kong

6789   490   98765432

Back cover: Above: Wild parakeet female with about three-week-old chicks; a pair of parakeets engaged in mutual preening; female parakeet taking a bath. Center: Two hand-tame young parakeets; wild parakeet female sitting in the entry hole of her nesting cavity. Below: Male parakeet grooming his tail feathers; parakeet in flight.

Photo credits
Bielfeld: page 73 (above, left); Effem (Society for European Communications): inside front cover, back cover (center, left); Martin: page 20 (below, right); Pforr; page 20 (above, left and right), inside back cover, back cover (above, right); Reinhard: pages 19, 38 (center, right, and below, right), 74, back cover (below, right); Reuter: page 38 (center, left); Ruckstuhl: page 38 (below, left); Scherz: page 38 (above, left); Scholtz: front cover, page 73 (above, right; below left and right); Schweiger: pages 100, 109, 110, 127, 128, back cover (above, left and center; center right); Trillmich: page 99; Wothe: pages 9, 10, 20 (below, left), 37, 38 (above, right), 55, 56, back cover (below, left).

Annette Wolter is an expert on birds who has kept small and large parrots for over thirty years. She is also the author of one of the most popular books in Barron's Pet Owner's Manuals: *Parakeets*. From her own extensive experience with parakeets and from the letters of her many readers Ms. Wolter has learned what care parakeets need and what parakeet owners most want to know. Communication with veterinarians, scientists of animal behavior, and breeders of parakeets keeps her up-to-date on all aspects of aviculture.

Dr. Immanuel Birmelin is a biologist and ornithologist at the University of Bern (Switzerland). For his doctoral thesis he studied parakeets intensively and wrote about the hatching of parakeet chicks and the behavior of the mother birds. Dr. Birmelin has been raising parakeets successfully for many years and still devotes a major portion of his scientific studies to these popular small parrots.

Table of Contents

3

Contents

Preface

This book deals with one of the most popular pets of our time, the parakeet or budgerigar. More than 45 million of these lively small parrots are kept in homes in the United States, Great Britain, Australia, and South Africa. With good care parakeets can live as long as ten to eighteen years, but few survive more than five years. What do we do wrong in looking after these pet birds?

Ornithologists and experts in animal behavior, who have explored this question in depth during the last ten years, have concluded that the habits of domesticated parakeets are still largely determined by the patterns of behavior inherited from their Australian ancestors. Wild parakeets live in large flocks and fly long distances at great speeds in their daily search for food. This means that adequate opportunity to fly and constant contact with other members of the species are vital needs of all parakeets. The birds we have as pets in our homes, however, are usually kept singly and often get far too little attention from their surrogate partners, i.e., their human owners; and only in exceptional cases are the birds allowed to fly around the house. Many keepers of parakeets do not know any better, and a number of misconceptions still prevail in spite of scientific knowledge to the contrary. Some mistaken notions are: If you want a parakeet that will become hand tame and learn to talk you have to keep a single bird. Or: Caged parakeets have no innate need for extensive flying.

This pet owner's guide puts an end to these and other misconceptions about the care of parakeets. Annette Wolter, a successful author of books on animals and an experienced keeper of parakeets, explains in detail how to keep these birds properly. You will find everything you need to know about acclimation, food, care, and everyday life with parakeets, whether you have a single bird, a pair, or a small flock. An extensive chapter explains what precautions help keep parakeets healthy and what you can do yourself if one of your birds should get sick.

Dr. Immanuel Birmelin, biologist, ethologist, and breeder of parakeets for many years, answers important questions on how to breed these birds. His descriptions of what happens inside the nesting box give an unprecedented glimpse of the family life of these lovable birds. He also explains how parakeets live in their native Australia and shows how they manage to survive in the Australian steppes and semi-deserts in spite of harsh climatic conditions. In addition, Dr. Birmelin points out patterns of behavior any keeper of parakeets can observe in his own birds. The insights gained through such observation can then help the aviculturist understand his birds better.

The drawings and color photos in this volume are informative and closely related to the text, many of them depicting interesting patterns of behavior characteristic of these intelligent small parrots.

The authors as well as the publisher would like to express their gratitude to everyone who has collaborated on this volume: the artist Fritz W. Köhler for his drawings that capture the special character of parakeets; the photographers, and especially Konrad Wothe, for the pictures—many of them new—of parakeets; and Messrs. Arendt and Schweiger, makers of animal films, some of whose exceptional shots of parakeets taken in Australia are published here for the first time. Finally, we should like to thank Fritz Trillmich, biologist at the Max Planck Institute for the Study of Animal Behavior at Seewiesen, for technical advice and for checking the manuscript.

Considerations Before You Buy

Does a Parakeet Fit Your Way of Life?

The parakeet is one of the most commonly kept cage birds. I am just as glad not to know how many hundreds of thousands of these creatures are forced to lead sad and unhealthy lives because their owners were unaware at the time of purchase what the needs of these highly developed birds are. The question of whether the buyers would meet these needs probably did not arise.

Friendly parakeets like to be in close physical contact with their keepers. Your hand, arm, or shoulder may become a favorite perch.

Before you decide to buy a parakeet you should be aware of how much one of these lively and sociable creatures could interfere with your way of life. Ask yourself realistically if you are prepared to take on this task.

I have summarized the most important points you should consider before buying a parakeet:
• If you want a parakeet as a friendly and tame pet you cannot leave the bird alone for hours on end every day. Days spent without company are incredibly long and dreary for such an active and sociable bird. If you work outside your home, is anyone else there during the day? Do you have children or a housemate who could at least spend some hours in the same room with the bird? Will this person pay attention to him (see page 32) or simply be an anonymous presence?
• If you decide to buy a pair of birds, they will probably try to raise a family. You should, therefore, have some idea of what to do with the young birds since you will probably not be able to keep them all yourself.
• A healthy parakeet can live from ten to eighteen years, and that is how long you will be responsible for the bird. It needs not just proper care and affection from anybody who is willing to provide it. Having formed a personal bond with you, your pet would go through deep mourning if it should be permanently separated from you.
• Meticulous care and a varied diet are essential to keep a parakeet healthy (see pages 46 and 52); both require an investment in time and money on the part of the keeper.
• Parakeets need things to keep them busy and plenty of opportunity to fly free. This means that the owner has to "bird-proof" the parakeet's room to prevent accidents (see List of Dangers, page 42).
• What will happen to your bird if you have to go on a trip or are forced to go to the hospital (see page 12)?

Considerations Before You Buy

• Do you have other pets? Are you sure a parakeet will fit in with them (see page 11)?
• Most people who buy parakeets hope that their pets will develop a talent for talking and whistling. Many parakeets do in fact say a number of words and phrases after a short time; they often imitate noises and learn quite a lot more, especially in the course of the first couple of years. But be aware that not every parakeet has an aptitude for imitating human speech. Some never even try; others prefer to whistle or settle for talking only parakeet talk for the rest of their lives. Ask yourself if your interest in the bird would vanish if it displayed no talent for speech.
• One other important point: A parakeet is not a suitable present, especially if it is a surprise gift. If you insist on giving a pet as a present because you think the recipient would truly enjoy having an animal, please express your generosity in the form of a "gift certificate." This way the recipient has a chance to decide at leisure whether and when to collect the gift. Anybody who acquires a pet should do so by choice and should freely assume the responsibilities that go along with the decision.

If you buy a parakeet for your children, be aware that without parents' active support children rarely are responsible enough to look after a bird on their own (see page 11).

One, Two, or More Birds?

Most pet parakeets are kept singly, and many of their owners assure me that their charges are content because they are given a lot of attention and are fed and cared for properly. Still, I am convinced that a parakeet that lives alone in captivity is not the creature it is meant to be. It will never have a chance to fulfill its inborn need for society by flying in a large flock, and it will never be able to perform that ritual (see page 86) programmed in its genes that precedes the formation of a lifelong bond with the chosen partner. To be sure, as a pet it will accept a human being as a surrogate partner and develop a tender attachment to this person, but in most cases the bird still has to spend many hours of the day alone, unable to engage in its natural activities, such as searching for food, flying for miles with the rest of the flock, looking for suitable sleeping places, warning others of potential enemies, and whatever else fills the day in the normal life of birds in the wild (see page 117).

Anyone deciding in favor of a single bird should have plenty of leisure and patience to make sure the pet will get all the attention it needs. If you live alone this is usually not so simple. A parakeet's instinctive need for sociability is perhaps met more easily by a family, assuming that all members enjoy spending time with the bird and are considerate of it. Even if all the family members play with the bird, the parakeet will probably pick a favorite and develop a special, close friendship with that particular person.

If you want your parakeet to be not only tame and responsive but also truly happy, you have to provide it with a partner. You may have been reluctant to start out with two birds, but you can still change your mind later (A Partner for Your Bird, page 34). This will afford you a double pleasure, namely, the pleasure of your personal friendship with them as well as the pleasure of observing the two birds. If you have not

Considerations Before You Buy

shared your home with a pair of birds, you cannot imagine how many charming facets of behavior two parakeets living together in captivity will display in their relationship. The birds exhibit amazing intelligence in overcoming inborn behavior patterns (e.g., in inhibiting aggression, see page 124), in trying to change the other one's mind about something, etc. One thing is clear: If you have two parakeets you can leave them alone for a day in good conscience, as long as their basic needs are taken care of. The birds may miss you because without you the "flock" is incomplete, but they won't suffer from loneliness and boredom.

It is possible to combine two male or two female birds; after a while they will learn to live quite happily together.

Of course, if you have a male and a female you will have the side benefit of a close-up look at parakeet family life. (Pages 80 to 104 give information on the breeding of these birds.) You should keep more than one pair only if you intend to breed birds on a regular basis. Because of their instinctive behavior patterns (see page 98) it is practically impossible to keep the birds from breeding. If your flock grows in size, it obviously needs more space. Work and demands on your time increase, and takers for the young birds will need to be found.

A fancier of parakeets ordinarily decides to keep a flock of birds only if living quarters offer enough space for a generous indoor aviary (see page 23) or if there is a garden where the birds can be housed in a large outdoor aviary.

Male or Female?

This question needs to be considered only if you are buying a mate for a bird that has up to now been kept singly. If you hope for baby birds you have to make sure that the bird you are about to buy is of the opposite sex from the one you already have (Tips on Buying Birds, page 14). If you are going to have only one parakeet, chances are that it will develop into a friendly, affectionate pet—perhaps even with a passion for chattering—whether it is male or female. Contrary to the persistent opinion that females are less likely to learn to talk and consequently do not become as tame as males, disposition, temperament, and talent for learning are in no way connected to sex. A healthy young parakeet—whether male or female—will learn everything within its capabilities if it is taught lovingly and patiently. Nobody can guarantee that a specific bird has a special talent for talking or will be exceptionally affectionate. The only difference between the sexes that generally holds true is that females seem to have a greater penchant for gnawing than males. This is not surprising because it is the female's natural task to choose the nesting cavity and, if necessary, work it to proper shape with her bill. If you provide a few branches (see page 17) or a bird tree (see page 31) this tendency to gnaw can be kept from becoming too much of a nuisance.

Two male parakeets. Two males can get along   ▷
very well; they engage in mutual preening and
often adopt the roles of "male" and "female."

Considerations Before You Buy

Children and Parakeets

Many children already have a pet parakeet or wish for one. There is nothing wrong with that as long as the parents know that the responsibility for the well-being of the pet cannot be left entirely to the child. With parental guidance most children will soon understand that an animal needs daily care and regular playtime. But the parents still have to be prepared to take over when the child "doesn't have time right now" because there is urgent school work to be done or because playing with friends is much more attractive than cleaning the dirty bird cage.

If you are considering getting a parakeet for your child, please remember that children often are inconsistent and may quickly lose interest in the pet they welcomed so ardently. When that happens they will not only grow neglectful of the chores but also stop spending time entertaining the bird. If you cannot revive the child's interest, perhaps by discussing the matter or by joining the child to observe and play with the bird, you yourself will have to take over the responsibility for the pet.

If your child wants an animal to hug and pet and is pleading for a dog, perhaps,

◁ Preening.
Above left: One bird scratches its partner's neck. Above right: The one that is being scratched twists its head so that the other bird can reach all the places in need of scratching. Below left: A parakeet cleans and smooths every little feather on the abdomen, too. Below right: To scratch its head a parakeet raises its leg from behind the wing.

please don't get a parakeet as a gesture of compromise. Even the tamest of parakeets that likes to have its head scratched cannot possibly satisfy a child's need for physical contact with an animal.

It is right and important for children to be around animals while growing up. This is the best way for them to learn love for animals and responsibility for another creature. But don't get a parakeet (or any other pet) just for the child; it should be a "family bird," for whose well-being all members of the household feel responsible.

Parakeets and Other Pets

A well-behaved dog that truly obeys its master will usually accept a parakeet as a new member of the family, unless the dog is being neglected in the general excitement over the newcomer. It is practically impossible, however, to get a cat and a bird to coexist peaceably, even though reports to the contrary suggest that in exceptional cases some animals learn to overcome their natural instincts. Other furred animals, such as hamsters, guinea pigs, or dwarf rabbits, do not make good company for parakeets because these animals, if kept in the same room, could harm birds by biting them and transmitting parasites to them.

If you keep your parakeets in a large aviary you can combine them with cockatiels, canaries, Java sparrows, or cordon-bleus. (Introduce the new birds in a separate compartment at first; don't overcrowd the aviary with birds.) Another suitable combination is a parakeet together with a cockatiel or a grey parrot.

Considerations Before You Buy

What to Do with Your Parakeet during Vacation

It is theoretically possible, but inadvisable, to take a parakeet along on a vacation if one travels by car and has room enough in it for the bird's accustomed cage. The long hours in the car, the summer heat, and the unfamiliar surroundings can do more damage to your pet's health (e.g., circulatory problems, diarrhea, colds caused by drafts) than a few weeks of separation. You would not be able to travel abroad with your bird, because almost all countries forbid the entry (and exit) of all kinds of parrots or, if they allow it, require endless forms to be filled out.

This means that you not only have to make reservations for yourself well in advance but also have to find a good place for your bird while you are gone. Not everybody has relatives or neighbors who can be safely entrusted with a bird (or other pets). The animal should be able to carry on its usual existence, which includes not only being fed and having fresh water and a clean cage but also the habitual privileges of free flying and some playtime with a person. It is cruel to make a parakeet that is used to periodic free flying sit in a locked cage for three or four weeks. A change of environment is upsetting enough in itself, causing many birds to grieve and lose interest in food. Make sure, therefore, to board your parakeet only where it will be given a chance to fly outside the cage and where the caretakers will take a genuine interest in it. If you cannot locate such a place you may be better off having someone come to your house once a day to look after the bird. This way it will not have to forego its daily

A pair of birds often indulge in mutual head scratching. This is part of preening and solidifies the bond between the pair.

period of free flying because, in the familiar and bird-proof surroundings of your home (see page 40), the cage door can be opened without risk. If you have a large aviary you have no choice but to arrange for someone to come in to look after the birds.

Some pet stores board parakeets. The cost is minimal, and the birds are usually well taken care of. (But just to be on the safe side you should have a careful look at where your pet will be housed.) Though this solution is convenient, I am reluctant to recommend it. I find it hard to imagine that parakeets that are used to "their" humans feel at ease surrounded by other birds, even if these are of the same species. The most well-meaning pet dealer will hardly have the time for a daily chat with every lonely "vacation guest." Free flying is obviously out of the question under these conditions.

There are other and better possibilities. In many cities, the Society for the Prevention of Cruelty to Animals or the local bird society has lists of people who are willing to take in animals temporarily. Anyone who is looking to place a pet or who would like to look after someone else's pet can inquire. If you are planning a trip, check in good time to see if someone will be available to adopt your parakeet temporarily. You will probably at least want to meet your substitute and make sure your pet will receive its accustomed care.

If there is no organization supplying such a service in your town, an ad in your local newspaper may help you find—often quite easily and quickly—a person who is knowledgeable about birds and willing to take over the care for one. Chances for finding someone are especially good if you offer to reciprocate.

A notice on the bulletin board of a church or a senior citizen center may also bring results, or an inquiry at a local university where students may be looking for odd jobs.

No matter who looks after your bird or birds, take the time to write down exactly what needs to be done: everything from feeding and normal bathing hours to time spent playing with the bird and letting it fly free in the room. The more concrete your instructions, the better the chances that you'll return to a healthy and, generally, quite cheerful pet.

There is one more question that has to be raised if the parakeet owner—particularly an older person—lives alone and keeps the bird as a companion to ward off loneliness. Although this is not a pleasant topic, any true lover of a pet will want to give thought to the fact that a day might come when care of the pet is no longer possible. A fall resulting in a broken hip, a slight stroke, or possibly sudden death would spell disaster for the bird if nobody is there to help. That is why any bird owner who lives alone should tell a neighbor about the bird and should arrange some method of signaling for help. The signal might be a newspaper still in the mailbox by noon, curtains closed longer than usual, or a certain object placed in the window at night and removed during the day if all is well. If you are reluctant to give away a key to your apartment, a neighbor could call the police if something seems to be the matter. Whatever the arrangement, there should be some written provision specifying what is to happen to the bird. If no "heir" is appointed, the parakeet could be taken to the nearest animal shelter. Many shelters have large community aviaries for escaped or abandoned birds.

Purchase and Housing

How to Go about Buying a Parakeet

If you have made up your mind that you want to buy a parakeet, look around with a critical eye in several pet stores. Are the birds kept in large enough and clean cages? Do they have sufficient food and fresh drinking water? Is there clean gravel on the bottom of the cages? All this will be the case at reputable pet dealers and well-managed pet sections of large department stores.

If a parakeet is startled or frightened it either jerks its head back slightly (left) or makes itself thin by stretching its body and flattening its feathers (right).

Perhaps you will have a chance to talk with a salesperson and find out something about the breeding background of the birds.

It is always better if you can avoid lengthy transport because a long trip is traumatic for the birds. If you do not find a bird that seems just right at a pet store, inquire at an aviculturists' association (see addresses, page 136) to see if there is a breeder of parakeets near where you live. You might get an address from the nearest animal shelter, or perhaps you will see a notice of a bird show where breeders exhibit their birds. At such an exhibition you can not only get addresses of breeders but you may also find out when a certain breeder expects his birds to have offspring and therefore when you can go and pick out a young parakeet.

I would strongly discourage you from buying a parakeet from a mail-order company. A bird that has undergone a long and uncomfortable journey is likely to arrive in a state of shock and possibly half-starved and dehydrated. If the miserable creature turns out to be sick or impaired you cannot simply mail it back. In other words, you've bought a pig in a poke. That is why I urge you to buy directly from a breeder or from a pet dealer; here you are likely to get good advice and reliable information.

Tips for Buying a Bird

No matter where you decide to buy your parakeet, you should know what to look for if you want to end up with a young and healthy bird. So-called "nest-young" (5-to-6-week-old) parakeets adjust more easily than older ones to human company as well as to members of their own species (important if you plan to introduce them to a partner). They become tame more quickly and usually develop more speaking proficiency. I do not mean at all to suggest that older parakeets cannot grow

14

into tame pets and good learners if treated with plenty of love and patience.

• Watch the bird of your choice for a while from a distance and observe its behavior. Is it active or is it sitting in a corner apathetically? Is it busy working on some object and interacting with other birds? Is it eating and drinking and preening itself? A lively and active parakeet will not long be subdued even by the change in surroundings when you bring it home and will soon start to respond to your overtures. A quiet and sleepy-looking bird, on the other hand, might be sick, though that is not necessarily the case. Perhaps it is just in a resting phase, and you should have another good look at it after a while.

• Pay close attention to the plumage of the parakeet. The feathers should hug the body smoothly and have a dull sheen. The ends of the tail feathers may be somewhat worn. This can be the result of transport, confined space in the nest, or some rough play with other birds. But the tail and wing feathers must be fully formed and should never be bent and stick out at an angle. If the feathers around the vent are dirty this suggests diarrhea, which may be a sign of temporary indisposition or real sickness.

• The feet and toes should be straight and clean. The two central toes point forward, the other two backward. The nails should not be too long, and the scales on the feet should form a smooth surface.

• You can tell a 5 to 6-week-old parakeet by its large, shiny, and perfectly round "button eyes," which do not yet show a light iris. In young birds, the wavy pattern of the neck feathers extends over the entire head of the ceres (the swellings at the base of the nostrils), and the spots of the throat are still

small or barely there at all. The bill of a young parakeet is darker than that of a fully grown one and often somewhat mottled; the ceres are still a light pink or beige in both sexes. In males, the ceres turn a bright blue after the juvenile molt, with the color intensifying during the courtship period (see page 86). The ceres of the female remain light beige past the juvenile molt but change when she gets ready to mate. They then turn brownish to dark brown and in some cases even get somewhat wrinkled.

There are exceptions to these rules: Albinos, i.e., white birds, have red rather than black eyes from the first; and in harlequin parakeets the ceres stay light beige into adulthood in males as well as females.

• You will simply have to trust the salesperson to catch the exact bird you have chosen from among the group in an aviary and that it will be a male or a female according to your desires. Only a true expert can reliably tell the sex of young parakeets, and there is only a small hint I can give you: Female parakeets have fine, hardly visible, light to whitish rings around the nostrils.

• Take one more look at the plumage around the vent while the salesperson is still holding your parakeet. Ask the clerk to blow at the feathers of this area so that you can see if the skin around the vent is red. This might mean that the bird is sick. Also run your finger gently over the bird's sternum (breastbone) to make sure it is rounded like the outside rim of a bowl. A collapsed sternum would indicate sickness.

• If you plan to participate in bird shows and your bird is not already wearing a band on its leg, ask a member of a budgerigaran society to put one on. However, bear in mind the injuries and trouble this band can cause. It can catch in something, and the bird may break its leg in an effort to get free. Or if the band gets too tight—which happens not infrequently since parakeets have strong, muscular legs—and you fail to notice it in time, circulation may be cut off, and in an extreme situation the leg may have to be amputated (see page 64). If you decide to have your bird banded (or leave a band that is already there), check regularly and make sure the bird is not hampered by the band. If, at any point, you decide to remove a band, have it done by an avian veterinarian.

The Right Bird Cage

Please keep in mind when you buy a cage that your parakeet's future home should not be a prison but a place of refuge where the bird can eat and sleep in safety. Pet stores have cages of many designs and in various sizes. If you buy a cage of the commonly offered sizes of 16 × 9 × 15 inches (41 × 23 × 38 cm) or 19½ × 10¼ × 10¾ inches (50 × 26 × 27 cm), your active parakeet will need several hours of free flying a day. Even with the best intentions of providing liberty by leaving the cage door open as much as possible you will have to keep your bird locked up many hours a day for its own safety (e.g., for airing the room, cleaning, parties). Your parakeet should be able to spread its wings in the space that is his home and at least flap them when moving from one end of the cage to the other. That is why I recommend that you invest in a larger cage and have a look at the so-called community cages.

A large bird cage in which a pair of parakeets can breed. The nest box with a top that opens is hanging in front of the side door.

You will find community cages measuring 27 × 14 × 19½ inches (69 × 36 × 50 cm) or 22½ × 12 × 22 inches (58 × 30 × 56 cm). These sizes are also suitable for a pair of birds and often come with a removable wire-mesh or plastic panel to subdivide the cage. Such a panel is useful if two birds are to get gradually acquainted with each other; for a single bird or a pair that is already used to living together the panel is superfluous.

The spaces between the bars of the cage walls should be no wider than ½ inch (12 mm), because with their agility parakeets can manage to squeeze through anything wider and get out of the cage quite easily.

Also make sure that the bars of at least two side walls of the cage run horizontally,

16

that the top of the cage is flat so that the bird can use it as a perch when outside the cage, and that the cage door can lock securely. Parakeets are clever, and they quickly learn to open a door if it can be done without too much trouble. If the locking mechanism gets loose through wear, the door should be secured with a small padlock, because all too many parakeets make their escape by opening the doors of their cages.

The "house" part of the cage is always mounted over a plastic bottom pan to keep gravel and empty seed hulls from being scattered. If you think you might want to raise young birds some day, make sure that the bars of the walls go all the way down into the pan so that fledgling birds not yet adept at flying can climb up again after landing on the bottom to pick up gravel or food. (Many cages have a removable tray; see drawing on page 16.) The tray should move easily in the bottom pan because it has to be taken out and put back every day.

If you want to do things right from the beginning and provide your parakeet with a home of ideal proportions—by this I mean a cage about 40 inches long, 20 inches deep, and 32 inches tall ($102 \times 51 \times 82$ cm)—the initial (nonrecurring!) cost is of course relatively high. You can save money if you build such a cage yourself; it is not very difficult and the materials are fairly inexpensive. Specialized dealers sell cage grating designed as front panels, which can be used in double lengths, if you wish. With them you can construct a large cage with three hardwood sides, a wooden floor, and a front of wire grating. Because it is open only on one side, such a "box cage" has to be placed where there is plenty of light. A better idea

would be a home-built cage with a wooden back and three sides of horizontal metal bars, which can be used for climbing. Parakeets have a great natural need for climbing.

Dealers also have plastic bottom pans for sale; trays used for developing film can also serve the purpose. For a cage about 40 inches long, two trays placed side by side are usually needed. Get the trays first and figure the dimensions of the cage on the basis of the tray size. Because the bottom pans have to slide in and out for cleaning, a hinged wooden clean-out flap that opens outward has to be located at the bottom of the front grating.

To save your buying the wrong cage let me mention types that are unsuitable for parakeets. Cages made of softwood or of woven wood will soon succumb to the tireless work of a parakeet's bill and then no longer safely contain the bird. Round cages fail to meet the needs of parakeets and other birds of the parrot family for a corner retreat. Pagodalike cages with gables and turrets are also inappropriate. These adornments are of no use to the bird and only hamper its freedom of movement, possibly cause injuries, and complicate your daily cleaning chores.

The Perches

No matter what kind of cage you buy, examine the perches closely. Proper perches are made of hardwood; plastic ones are less desirable. The perches should not all be of the same diameter. That places a strain on the bird's feet because they get no chance to use different muscles. Perches are of comfortable thickness if the bird's toes reach around them without the claws touching. But in nature birds do not use only branches of the exact right size. The change from quite thin to very thick branches offers the muscles of the feet the necessary exercise. For resting and sleeping, your parakeet will automatically choose a branch of a comfortable size. Replace at least two of the original perches with three or four natural branches of different thicknesses. Branches from oak trees, alders, poplars, mountain ash, or fruit trees are suitable. Avoid trees that have been exposed to auto exhaust or that have been sprayed with insecticide. Yew trees, which are poisonous, are of course disqualified. Branches have to be trimmed to size and solidly mounted inside the cage in such a way that they do not interfere too much with the parakeet's freedom of movement. The branches will be gnawed to pieces in time and should then be replaced with fresh ones.

Most parakeet cages come equipped with a swing and often with a ladder as well. The swing usually becomes the bird's favorite spot where it especially likes to spend the night. If you have two birds in one cage you may want to buy a second swing, but make sure the two birds don't get into each other's way when they use the swings. The ladder is a different story. Many birds never make use of it, and it only takes up space. If your bird doesn't use the ladder, take it out. This gives the bird more room in the cage and saves you some cleaning.

Food and Water Dishes

Food and water dishes come with the cage as part of its basic equipment. But if you keep two birds in one cage you may want to get a second set to prevent competition. For offering supplemental foods, pet dealers have available practical semi-oval dishes that can be hung on the horizontal bars (see drawing on page 49). You can mount these dishes near the top perches so that the food in them is less likely to be contaminated by droppings. The food and water dishes on the bottom should have plastic shields to protect them from droppings from above. If these dishes lack shields, you can mount the perches in such a way that the birdseed and water stay clean or you can hang more semi-oval dishes near the uppermost perches.

Automatic water and food dispensers— usually in the form of small plastic containers mounted on the outside of the cage but with small trays for the water or seeds reaching inside the cage—have the great advantage of keeping food and water clean (see illustration on page 52). These gadgets are especially useful if you have to leave your bird for a day or two without anyone to feed it. It is obviously essential that the bird be familiar with these food and water

Parakeets are fast and adept flyers. If a bird is to ▷ remain healthy it needs a lot of free flying time in the house.

dispensers. Many parakeets learn to use them the first time they are introduced to them, but others cannot deal with them or are too scared of them to use them. Parakeets have died of hunger or thirst when their owners were away even though there was plenty of food and water in the dispensers. That is why it is important to leave the familiar dishes with food and water in the cage when the automatic dispensers are first introduced and until the birds have become accustomed to them.

Useful Accessories

Pet stores offer a number of accessories that are useful or necessary for the care of a parakeet.
• A bath house is the most important item. The best kind is one that can be hung in the opened cage door and that has a cover. It is essential that the floor be grooved or have some raised pattern so that the bird will not slip in the water. A bird that has slipped is not likely to show interest in a bath for some time to come, if ever. Maybe your bird will first react with fright to this unfamiliar thing that has suddenly appeared

◁ Active parakeets.
Above left: A female bird is taking a bath. Above right: A curious female is investigating a ballpoint pen. Below left: A female is hanging head down trying to drive her partner off the perch of the nest box. Below right: A male sitting on a climbing branch.

A bath house that can be hung in the opening of the cage door. The textured surface of the bottom is important because if the bottom is smooth, the birds slip while bathing.

and blocks the exit. But in time your pet will get used to the installation and may even enjoy taking a sip of the water before diving in. The bath house should be filled with about one inch of lukewarm water. If the bird still refuses to bathe after repeated offers, try placing in the water some wet greens (spinach, dandelion leaves, or lettuce, but only vegetables grown in a home garden; see page 48). Perhaps your parakeet prefers this way of getting wet to a thorough soaking. Apart from the kind of bath houses just described, there are also smaller models that are made of plastic and usually have a mirror in the bottom. But these are much too small; when parakeets take a bath, they like to spread out one wing at a time and dip its underside in the water.

If your parakeet's tastes run more in the direction of a light sprinkling, never use a plant sprayer that might at some time have contained a pesticide. Many parakeets like

21

to drink water and take baths by standing under a slowly dripping faucet. But always check that the water coming from the faucet is lukewarm. You can easily tell when a parakeet wants not only to quench its thirst but also to get wet. The excited fluffing up of the feathers is the bird's way of asking for a shower.

• Climbing hoops to fit any type of cage are sold and can be mounted above the top of the cage. Usually they have a little bell, a mirror, or a few wooden steps at the center. The toy is unimportant, but the hoop offers the bird one more chance for activity as well as an additional surface to land on.

• For the inside of the cage you can buy ladders, swings, rings of plastic or wood, bells, mirrors, plastic parakeets, and more. But before you clutter the bird's quarters, buy just one item at a time and see if your bird actually uses it. If not, remove it, because elbow room is more crucial to the bird's happiness than a useless toy.

The Right Spot for the Cage

The cage should be permanently located in the room where the bird's owner, or the family, spends the most time. However, a kitchen is not a good place, because cooking vapors, especially from frying, are harmful. Necessary airings easily result in drafts and big fluctuations in temperature. In addition, a kitchen is full of hazards, such as hot burners, pots filled with hot things, open windows, pans full of liquids (dishwater covered with soap suds is easily mistaken for a landing surface), empty containers a bird can slide into, open cupboard doors and drawers, etc. (see List of Dangers on page 42). If the kitchen is the center of activity, the bird, too, has to be given a place there, but the parakeet must be supervised very carefully.

Whether the cage is located in the kitchen or the living room, it should be assigned a permanent place at an adult's eye level, perhaps on a bureau of the right height, on a shelf, or on a special bird-cage stand. This spot should not be like a traffic island. The ideal place is a bright corner from which the parakeet can survey its surroundings and the various activities around it and get used to things without feeling bothered or threatened. To feel really safe, birds like to have protection from behind; the back of the cage should therefore be right up against a wall so that only three sides are "exposed." A window sill is not suitable because it is too low, the window radiates cold in the winter, and the direct sun in the summer can cause heat stroke. Sunshine is healthy for birds, but not when the heat is intensified through glass. In any case, the bird should always have a chance to retreat into the shade. The location of the cage should also be free of vibrations. A spot on the refrigerator, the washing machine, the dishwasher, or even the TV is therefore out of the question. Nor should the cage face the TV screen, because the flickering of light and dark makes a parakeet nervous, and birds need to be quiet in the evening. When the TV is on, be sure the sound is not too loud.

If possible, avoid activities above the cage like putting away or looking for things on high shelves or in high cupboards. Parakeets have an instinctive fear of anything that happens above their heads, because in the wild there is always a danger of predator

Purchase and Housing

A stand for a small parakeet cage with a gravel tray that slides out on the side. With a cage this size a parakeet needs lots of free flying.

birds swooping down from above. It will be easiest to find a bright but relatively protected spot for your bird if you buy a stand from which the bird cage hangs free (only suitable for small cages, see illustration on page 23). But you have to make sure that the bottom of the stand is heavy enough so that the cage is not likely to topple over.

Periodically check the screw that holds the arched metal pipe to the base of the stand; the screw can work itself loose and must then be tightened to insure the balance of the cage. With a hanging cage it is also important to reinforce the two clamps holding the bottom pan to the body of the bird cage. These clamps tend to get loose in the course of time, and one day the bottom might drop to the floor. This would scare the bird half to death and also necessitate a lot of cleaning up for the bird's owner. That is why you should attach small S-hooks to these clamps (or to the lowermost crossings of the wire bars). Stretch a wide rubber band between the two hooks so that the rubber band hugs the bottom of the tray and provides extra support. You will need to replace the rubber band every few months because it will lose its elasticity.

Important: The parakeet will come to accept its immediate surroundings as home and feel most comfortable there. If it is necessary to move the bird to other places, this should be done only gradually and always after making sure that these other locations meet the necessary requirements.

Aviaries

If you want to keep several parakeets or a mixed flock, you will need an aviary, i.e., a space large enough to allow the birds to fly short distances. The large cages described on page 16 are too small for even two pairs of birds, especially with the appearance of baby birds, which in time have to be able to practice flying (see page 93). A small aviary (see illustration on page 24) will accommodate two to three pairs comfortably and be

Purchase and Housing

A movable small aviary in which several parakeets can live together. Two pairs can breed simultaneously in such an aviary.

If your dwelling is sufficiently spacious you can provide your birds with generous living quarters by turning a bright, draft-free corner of a room into an aviary (see illustration on page 41). If you are handy with tools you can accomplish this yourself without much trouble, especially since you can buy prefabricated panels of grating or mesh. Such an aviary need not be very deep (3 to 4½ feet) but should be wide—as wide, in fact, as possible. When you set up an aviary you should follow the same rules that apply to setting up a cage (see pages 16 to 22).

Parakeets reproduce readily and in an aviary of good size will sit on eggs and raise their young without problems. Many a fancier of parakeets who started out with a few birds in an indoor aviary has ended up keeping the birds in the garden. Limited space usually forces the hobby breeder to take the next step and move the operation outdoors. For building an outdoor aviary I have to refer the reader to specialized literature where exact instructions on the construction of outdoor aviaries of all sizes are given. But there is one point that I do want to mention here: If you plan and build an outdoor aviary, it *has to* include a shelter that can be heated. Parakeets do survive temperatures below freezing, but at what cost! If they have to spend a long, cold winter without proper shelter they merely vegetate. They may stay alive, but it can hardly be called living. In their native Australia parakeets experience temperatures comparable to our winters only for a few hours in the night, not for days and weeks on end.

spacious enough for the birds to raise young. These aviaries are available in different models, some of them very decorative (anything from aluminum to wooden trim, and, in some cases with a cabinet for a base). Because of limited space few pet stores carry these aviaries, and you will have to order from a catalog. As a rule, a pet dealer will advise you well and help you choose the model that best suits your particular needs.

Keeping and Caring for Parakeets

Transport and Arrival at the New Home

You are at the pet store, and your parakeet is sitting in a small cardboard box, ready for the trip home. The box is equipped with a few air holes. Your bird is not panicked at this point; instead it feels quite cozy, as though transported back to its early days in the nest. But it is important that it has enough air to breathe, so the box should not be put in a plastic bag. The best way to carry the box is in your hands. Keep it from being jostled and protect it from the cold, perhaps by holding your coat around it loosely. Now get the bird home as quickly as you can. Everything there should be ready and set for the first twenty-four hours. The cage should stand in the chosen spot, the bottom tray covered with bird gravel, a dish filled with fresh drinking water and another with a birdseed mixture. A spray of millet might be clamped to the cage wall near a perch as a welcoming treat. Now the box in which the parakeet arrived is opened on one side and held in front of the open cage door, but without leaving any crack for escape. The bird is probably ready to emerge from its dark "nest" into the light and thus moves into its new home. If it should hesitate, start tilting the box until the bird begins to slide and thus lands in the cage. Shut the door carefully and leave the bird alone for the next few hours. Provided with everything it needs, it can eat and drink, inspect its new quarters, and have a look at its surroundings without any people to distract and frighten it.

The young parakeet will be filled with fear all the same. This is the first time in its life that it is not with fellow nestlings or others of its kind. It may show apprehensiveness by squatting timidly in a corner of the cage floor or by sitting on a perch facing the wall, but curiosity may soon get the better of the youngster and it will start looking around. Now it is up to you whether its first experiences in the new environment are positive or negative. Once the bird pecks at the birdseed, has a sip of water, then preens itself and starts moving around, the worst is over.

Try to avoid anything during the first few days and weeks that might put your parakeet into a state of discomfort or panic, such as:
• Constant activity near the cage, slamming of doors, and other noise.
• Abrupt movements, loud talking, screaming, and quarreling nearby.
• Glaring light in the evening; only soft light should reach the cage.
• Direct exposure to a television screen; TV sound that is turned up high. (The shooting in murder mysteries is especially frightening to birds.)
• Loud music or screaming voices coming from a radio.
• Garish or dark colors in clothing; many parakeets show fear when they see something black.
• Appearing suddenly before your bird with a startling hat on or in curlers; this could be frightening.

The First Few Weeks with the Bird

During the first few days you should not get too close to the cage but should keep talking with your parakeet in a soft voice. Always say the bird's name when you enter the room or approach the cage. It is especially important to talk to the bird soothingly the

25

first few times you do the necessary daily chores of replacing gravel, water, and birdseed. If you see that your parakeet likes spray millet, give a little piece every day (see page 50). Once the bird puts up with your activities in its cage without fluttering about or any other signs of nervousness, offer a little spray millet with your hand at the same time every day. Stay very quiet at first and don't get too close; hold the millet so that the bird can just reach it from its perch without having to touch the hand that still evokes fear. Gradually hold it differently so that the parakeet first puts one foot on the spray in your hand and later, as the bird becomes more relaxed, takes the treat from your hand, maybe even perching on it.

When you set up the cage for your parakeet, include a small brass bell that hangs from the roof by a short chain. Such a bell is most likely to be accepted as a surrogate companion because it is small and nonthreatening. The metal surface shows the parakeet some reflection, making a single bird feel less lonely. The parakeet can also play

Toys for parakeets: a ball with an attached bell, a rolling toy, a playing ball with a small bell inside it, and a toy figure made of softwood.

with the bell, making it ring, pulling on the chain, or using its bill to nudge the bell like a fellow bird. Once the bell has become a trusted toy you may want to use a second one to lure your pet to your hand or shoulder.

An Undisturbed Night's Rest

Parakeets have a sense of tradition. Activities that have proved pleasant and without threat become habits that are then obstinately defended against change. Your parakeet, too, is bound to develop certain routines that you should respect. First of all it will decide on a permanent sleeping place. When it gets tired in the evening and its interest in surrounding activities wanes, it will retire to its chosen spot, tuck its bill into its back feathers, and probably pull up one leg close to its body. Maybe you'll hear a last, contented peep, and soon the bird will be asleep. Before turning off the light in the evening, you should give your bird a chance to retire to its sleeping place. After that the bird should not be startled by loud and unfamiliar noises. Muted sounds that occur every evening will not bother it. It will be aware of these sounds, but because they are normal they are no cause for alarm. If the room where the bird cage is located is used late into the evening, if people are smoking and watching TV, or if bright lights are on, the cage should be covered with a light cloth to give the bird some protection. But the cloth should not darken the cage altogether. In case the bird is suddenly startled it is better if there is some dim light to help the parakeet orient itself. Otherwise it may blindly try to get away, fluttering wildly in its cage and possibly injuring itself. If the room is not used in the evening, there is no need to cover the cage unless a street light is shining brightly through the window. If you do cover the bird at night you have to remove the cloth at daybreak, because birds, with their fast metabolism, have to start eating and drinking early after the night's rest. (Make sure there is enough food left in the dishes for morning.) Parakeets need as much daylight as possible, and short winter days call for some additional hours of artificial light.

Habit plays an important role in a parakeet's life as a pet. If someone normally sleeps in the same room, for instance, the bird will get used to the noises produced by the sleeper, and these will not disturb the bird at night. But if it has to share the room with another creature—whether human or animal (e.g., another bird visiting)—just for once, your parakeet may wake up in the middle of the night and start fluttering around in a panic. Under such unusual circumstances it is best to provide some light near the cage with a 15-watt bulb, so that the bird can reassure itself that there is no danger and settle down again. Loud, unexpected noises, as from passing cars, can also lead to nighttime panic. As soon as you become aware of this, briefly turn on the light in the bird's room and calm the bird in a soft voice.

Winning Your Bird's Trust

Since parakeets lead nomadic lives in their natural environment, they are adept and powerful flyers (see page 29). No living room is large enough to accommodate their flying needs and skills. To make up for this lack, your bird should at least have the opportunity to practice climbing, at which a parakeet is also a born artist, and be given suitable objects to work over with its untiring bill.

But let us return to your parakeet's first few days in your home. Once it has lost its initial fear of you—by "you" I mean the person who looks after the bird from the first day on, spends the most time with it, and observes it with loving attention—you can begin to get it used to your hand. The first role in which your pet gets to know you is as a provider of food. Try even during the first few days to introduce parsley, spinach leaves, pieces of apple or carrot, strawberries, grapes, slices of banana, or tangerine sections. Once the bird is used to this supplemental food you will soon notice what it is especially fond of, and you can start spoiling it with healthful treats. Setting up a consistent routine is also part of making it feel comfortable. A parakeet quickly knows what time it is given fresh food in the morning, what time you bring its favorite special treat, and when you come to spend some time with it quietly, talking to it softly or whistling something for it to imitate, or bring its little bell to serve as surrogate company. Allow the bird to initiate greater closeness. Remain a passive presence, provide your company patiently, offer a tasty morsel from your hand, tentatively suggest a game.

Watch to see what habits the bird adopts and help when you can. If your parakeet tries, for instance, to take a bath in its water bowl, hang the bath house, filled with ¾ of an inch of lukewarm water, in the cage door opening. Of course the bird will first shy away from this strange object and be too cautious to think of bathing. Put the bath house up every other day, perhaps with a small bunch of parsley in the water. Birds like parakeets that live in desertlike areas often take their morning bath in the dew-wet grass and don't necessarily need a real bath.

If you observe your bird busily hacking to shreds a piece of carrot stuck between the bars without eating any of it, attach a section of washed and dried elderberry branch to the cage in such a way that the bird can gnaw on it. But always keep patient. Parakeets are cautious and mistrustful of all innovations. You may have to offer a number of delicious strawberries that will go untouched before your bird dares eat a seed off the fruit. And many a toy that later becomes the focus of passionate interest is initially regarded with suspicion and ignored until one day it is pecked at and used. Careful observers often notice how a parakeet will, after a quick shudder, shake out all its feathers and then calmly proceed to look over something new or put up with an overture at closeness. This shaking of the feathers indicates relaxation after agitation. A parakeet gets excited or agitated often for all kinds of reasons and to different degrees, but after shaking its feathers it becomes calm again, and it may often be ready for new ventures and discoveries.

The reason for a bird's agitation often remains a mystery to the observer, and it is even harder to understand why a bird will sometimes fly up in a panic as though trying to escape from some invisible danger. This quick, frightened flight often ends in an emergency landing on a perch that is never otherwise used or on some ordinarily shun-

ned object. All you can do at this point is to talk softly and soothingly to your bird. Unfortunately we have no idea what makes a parakeet go through these apparently pointless motions of flight reaction.

A bird shaking its feathers. You will see your parakeet do this several times a day. It puffs up its feathers briefly and then shakes its entire body.

Keeping and Caring for Parakeets

The First Flying Hours

The proper time to let a parakeet leave its cage for the first time depends entirely on how well it has adjusted to you and its surroundings. If it no longer flutters around excitedly when you do things in its cage and no longer turns stiff and slim with fear when you approach, you can open the cage door. But make sure all room doors and windows are safely shut. Even an open window behind venetian blinds can serve as an escape route to a parakeet that has decided to take off. Curtainless windows often spell disaster. Not being able to see the glass, a bird may fly straight toward the light and crash against the window. Death by a broken neck or skull may be the sad result. If you have no curtains of any kind in front of your windows you will have to teach your bird that the window is a boundary. Cover the window except for about 12 inches at the bottom by lowering shades or by some other method and turn on the electric light in the room if it is too dark otherwise. The uncovered portion at the bottom of the window can then be increased a couple of inches every day. This way the bird learns to respect the window as the "end of its world."

Be sure to stay in the room and watch your parakeet when you open the cage door. Perhaps the bird first hovers in the cage because the unaccustomed opening arouses suspicion. But it may quickly grasp your intention and cautiously climb up on the outside of the cage to get a better view of things from the top. Then, quickly or after some hesitation, your bird will take off. In the air for the first time, it may be seized by anxiety at the sight of all the new and untested landing opportunities. Perhaps it will find its way back to the cage on this first outing and return there, but it is more likely to fly higher and land on a tall shelf, a curtain rod, or a lamp. There the bird will sit, panting with agitation. First it needs to calm down. Relief is on the way if it shakes its feathers; and if it starts tripping around on this new perch, peering around curiously and even preening itself, it has conquered the worst fear. Now you should talk to the bird, saying its name in a praising tone, but don't under any circumstance interfere actively. All the bird needs is some time to muster the courage to fly back. This may take a while, and even now it may not make it back to the cage. But the bird has now seen the cage, and sooner or later the bird will find its way back. If this does not happen, bring the opened cage up close to the bird after about half an hour. It will no doubt be ready to exchange its perch for the safety the cage represents and conclude the exciting adventure by eating a few seeds. If the parakeet should land on the floor—which is quite likely if thus far in its young life it has had little opportunity to fly—you can spoil the bird a little by tossing a few seeds on the floor from a little distance. As soon as the bird notices this it will hop from one seed to the next. This way of eating appeals greatly to a parakeet because it is how these birds get food when living wild in the steppes, where they gather grass seeds from the ground (see page 117).

No matter how the first session of free flying ends, don't make the mistake of waving brooms or cloths at the bird in an effort to dislodge it from a high retreat in order to return it to its cage. Such an experience would convince it that you are its enemy from whom it has to try to get away. If everything else fails, leave the bird sitting where it is overnight. If it is hungry the next morning it will pick up its courage for the return flight or hop into the cage held up to it. If there is some compelling reason why the bird should not spend the night outside the cage, wait until evening and then grab the bird in the darkened room and gently return it to the cage. After all, you want your pet to think of you as a friend in need and develop trust in you.

Of course this first flying venture must not be a one and only experience. Your bird should have an opportunity to fly extensively every day, preferably at the same hour. As it is, a parakeet can make only very limited use of its excellent, inborn flying skills in our small living spaces. In nature these birds are not only strong but also extremely fast flyers, even exceeding the speed of swallows.

Life with a Parakeet

The safer and happier your parakeet feels with you, the more aggressively it will try to satisfy its curiosity, its longing for companionship, and its urge to keep busy. If, however, you keep your bird locked up all day except for the daily flying sessions, you will soon have a dull, sleepy bird that succumbs to lethargy caused by the monotony of limited movement within the cage and by playing the same old games over and over with lifeless things. When released from the cage your pet will still fly back and forth, perch on your shoulder, and court you by eagerly nodding its head, but this liveliness will disappear with the return to the cage because one short hour of freedom is not enough to prevent the dulling of spirit. The parakeet will gradually lose the ability to make use of its many-sided talents.

But if you let the bird move freely in the room, it may attack wallpaper, posters, books, and papers with a passion, decorating them with innumerable chomp marks. Female parakeets keep especially busy with their bills and can cause extensive damage to any material fit for chewing on (see page 8). However, with a little bit of effort you can protect your belongings against this destructive tendency of parakeets. If the wallpaper is within easy reach from a favorite perch, that section of paper can be covered with sturdy plastic, cardboard, or a thin board. Or small branches can be used to distract the bird's attention from the wall. Bookshelves can be covered with cloths temporarily, while a couple of books you don't care about are sacrificed and put in a spot where the bird is allowed to chew on things. Usually the bird starts losing interest in this rather boring "job" anyway and is unlikely to return to the bookshelves. With the typical inventiveness of a parakeet it will set out in search of new tasks.

Needless to say, the bird will leave behind traces of its presence—regularly deposited droppings—outside the cage wherever it likes to spend time in the room. The only thing you can do about it is to let the droppings dry and then vacuum them up or to cover the floor beneath their favorite perches. These small daily problems can be avoided, however, if you create an appropriate living center for the parakeet outside its cage, namely a parakeet tree.

Keeping and Caring for Parakeets

The Parakeet Tree

Give over a square yard of your living room to the parakeet and set up a climbing tree (see illustration at right). Use as large and heavy a bucket as you can and fill it with potting soil. The bucket should be a good three feet in diameter to serve its purpose. Plant three to four long, sturdy branches vertically in the bucket and connect them at two or three levels with horizontal branches of varying thickness and shape. To tie the branches together you can use strips of bast, the ends of which have been thinly covered with a nontoxic glue for longer wear. Place some potted vines in the bucket between the vertical branches. These lend the "tree" some extra support and make it look more attractive. Unfortunately even biologists and botanists cannot always be relied on to know which house plants are toxic for parakeets. But from experience I know that oleander, some primroses, hyacinths, and yew are poisonous for parakeets, whereas kangaroo vine (cissus), hibiscus, and ferns are not. (For poisonous plants, see List of Dangers on page 42.)

The potting soil is covered with a layer of bird gravel, which allows you to remove droppings easily with a slotted spoon without having to replace the gravel very often. What is really important in building the bird tree is the length of the horizontal branches. They should not stick out beyond the rim of the bucket, because otherwise the droppings land around the bucket instead of in the gravel. This is because birds like best to sit on the ends of the branches.

All the parakeets I know that have a bird tree as a living space like to spend time there and leave the room's furnishings

A parakeet tree made of bamboo sticks and natural branches. You can construct a tree like this yourself and it will soon become your bird's favorite place.

alone. They return to the cage for eating and drinking and some of them for sleeping, though many also spend the night in the tree. Of course the birds don't just climb from branch to branch but also chew on the branches and on the ties. But that, after all, is the purpose of the tree. The branches have to be renewed from time to time. Collect them from the woods or a garden, not along the roadside where trees and shrubs are exposed to poisonous exhaust

31

fumes. If you use branches from fruit trees make sure they have not been sprayed with pesticides. To be safe, thoroughly spray all branches with hot water and let them dry before using them.

Toys and Other Ways to Keep Your Bird Busy

All kinds of toys are sold to meet the parakeet's instinct for play, many of which are hardly used for their intended purpose. For a single parakeet these items often serve less as toys than as a surrogate partner. What your parakeet needs more than anything else for play is your company. A parakeet will entertain itself, for instance, by rolling a marble, a ball with a bell inside it, or a stand-up toy around on a table and shoving the toy off the edge to watch with fascination as it drops. If someone picks up the toy so that it can be knocked off again, the parakeet will go on playing with unflagging interest. Parakeets often enjoy carrying a ball with a bell in it all the way across the table and then dropping it over the edge. Take enough time to play with your parakeet and you will come to admire its agility, delight in play, and inventiveness. The nature of the toy is secondary. Something that rolls straight is excellent. Roll it gently toward the bird. If it comes too fast he will make way for it timidly, run away, and then, turning suddenly, kick it away. This can turn into a fun game that will hold not only the bird's attention but yours as well. Parakeets also like to play with a little bell, running toward it and giving it a good shove with the bill, then dodging it quickly as it swings back. A small bell inside a globe

of plastic netting can even serve as a miniature device for exercise. My parakeet used to like to sit on the top branch of his tree with the toy in his beak and then flip it down with a toss of the neck. My role was to catch the toy and return it. But many a time I had to stoop down to pick it up off the ground because the clever bird had tried to make me miss the catch. It was obvious that my pet found it much more entertaining when I was made to stoop.

When a parakeet stretches one leg backward this is a sign of well-being and comparable to our stretching in relaxed comfort.

If you don't have much inclination to play with your parakeet like this, it will almost inevitably turn favorite objects into surrogate partners. At an animal clinic I watched a female parakeet in an isolation cage huddle up to a shot glass in an effort to comfort herself in her loneliness. A plastic parakeet that can be attached to a perch quite obviously serves as a surrogate partner. It will be an object of affection as it is billed and fed, but then it is also kicked and beaten. The beating is a result of sheer desperation, because the live bird has done everything it can think of to woo the other, and the plastic bird never responds. The surrogate nature of activities with other objects is not quite so clear, but one can often observe a parakeet raising its head feathers, narrowing its pupils to pin holes, and giving vent to its excitement with a soft growl as it coos over a toy or bows eagerly before it.

A little ball made of plastic mesh can prompt a bird to go through the motions of mating. The bird grabs the ball with both feet and rubs his vent on the ground, often until a sexual secretion appears.

This brings us to the mirror, an item present in almost any parakeet cage and also the focus of heated debate. I find myself in conscious disagreement with biologists who object to a mirror as a surrogate partner for a parakeet. They say having a mirror around is unnatural for birds and makes them sick. But a parakeet living in captivity is by necessity deprived of a natural life. The bird has to make do with human beings, confined living space, and surrogate activities. In addition parakeets naturally form lifelong monogamous bonds with their partners and are predisposed to living in flocks (see page 116). Even if a pet parakeet finds a surrogate partner in human shape, the problem of its sexuality remains unsolved. The bird's mirror image not only consoles during hours of loneliness but it also offers a chance to satisfy social needs. To be sure, the mirror evokes sexual impulses, but a healthy parakeet is sexually active even without it and simply chooses other surrogate objects for the same purpose. Besides, you simply cannot ban everything with a reflecting surface from a living room. Somewhere the bird will find a shiny object that throws back its image, which will be regarded as another parakeet. I would let even a pair of birds have a mirror to give them the illusion of being part of a flock. Anyone who objects to a mirror and the reactions it evokes as unnatural would, to be consistent, have to be opposed to keeping parakeets altogether unless a flock could be housed in a large aviary.

Do All Parakeets Learn to Talk?

Many parakeets need no special encouragement to start whistling, imitating sounds, or saying words they hear a lot. But interest and talent for mimicry varies from parakeet to parakeet. Some give veritable concerts by copying the voices of songbirds, and others can fool you with their imitations of a ringing telephone, a creaking door, or screeching car brakes. Many birds like to focus their talents on repeating words and phrases, but some are content to stay with the natural chirping and twittering of their species. Don't be disappointed if your parakeet is among the latter. The bird may develop other talents that have just as much charm. But if you notice that your bird is starting to chatter and tries to say words, it is worth your while to be patiently encouraging.

The old wives' tale that a bird's tongue needs to be loosened before it will begin to talk is sheer nonsense and can give rise to cruelty to animals. All the so-called talking pills that are sold in Europe may be tasty to parakeets, but they have no influence whatsoever on the gift for speech. If a parakeet shows talent and an interest in talking this is because it wants to "have its say" in the company of humans—its new flock—and because it wants to belong. Besides, saying words the bird has heard occupies it during idle hours. A parakeet interested in talking will sit in the hand of its human friend, edging as close as possible to the person's mouth and listening entranced to the words spoken. If the person does it right the parakeet keeps learning new words and combinations. The bird likes to hear over and over the expressions it already knows, and as new words are introduced to the vocabulary already mastered they are eagerly tried out and repeated. If this special intimacy between bird and human remains undisturbed, the parakeet is most likely to learn the new words without getting distracted. The bird would like nothing better than to indulge in this intimate talk several times a day, but most bird lovers don't have this kind of time. I have solved the problem by resorting to a tape cassette. My parakeet could hardly get enough of listening to the entire repertoire on the tape while lying belly down on the small speaker.

Parakeets often use words and phrases correctly in an appropriate context. One of my parakeets was inordinately timid at first, and every time I had to blow my nose, I had to warn the bird so that it would not be too frightened. I would say "Excuse me, I'm going to blow my nose." Later on the bird produced this sentence every time I reached for my handkerchief. When we played together I said much too often "My little sweetheart, my little sweetheart." When this male parakeet later cooed with his mate, I would hear these words repeated every time.

But I must admit that if your pet does not happen to have an exceptional gift the speech lessons require a lot of patience. You have to say the words you want learned hundreds of times. By the way, the commonly held assumption that females are less interested in learning to talk does not apply to birds kept singly. But if the female lives together with a male she turns her attention to other tasks and lets the male do the talking.

A Partner for Your Bird

Even if you refuse to believe at first that a pair of parakeets is easier to keep and happier than a single one, you may be convinced in time as you get more familiar with your bird and see how active and gregarious a creature it is. How many hours a day does the parakeet have to spend without company? If you watch your pet at these times you can't fail to notice how uninterested and sad it looks as it sits there doing nothing. No bird keeps busy every minute from morning to night; there are always moments of rest alternating with business. But a parakeet needs a partner to share all its doings, including rest and sleep. All birds that live in flocks are stimulated to activity by their partners and by the other birds around them (see page 118). If one bird starts preening itself, soon all the others will be busy cleaning their plumage. If one flies off in search of food, most of the rest will follow. If one wants to rest and sleep, its partner, if no other bird, will get sleepy too. There is much we humans can do for a parakeet. We can play with it, talk to it, coo over it, and scratch its head when it asks by stretching its head toward us. A male parakeet may even become so attached to a human partner that he will be aroused to

Keeping and Caring for Parakeets

In the course of courtship display a male parakeet feeds his female partner to get her into mating mood, but rubbing beaks is also a favorite activity outside of the mating period.

perform the motions of copulation. But in the end we have to admit that we cannot communicate with him in his "mother tongue." In no way are we able to reciprocate his affections with the proper nuances a partner of his species naturally displays.

If you take all this into consideration there is hardly any excuse for not getting your parakeet a mate. The previous hesitations are understandable: Will a bird that has a mate still maintain friendship with you, play with you, fly to meet you and greet you happily, keep up the cheerful

chattering? A lot depends on timing. If the first parakeet has already developed the kind of trustful relationship to you that I have described, nothing much will change. A companion of its own species will enrich the parakeet's life but hardly represents a reason to give up treasured habits. On the contrary, the newcomer will learn from the first parakeet that life with humans is tolerable. With luck and patience you will end up with two tame and affectionate parakeets, although the first bird will always claim special rights in its relationship to you.

If your first parakeet was still young when it arrived, several months or as much as a year might have passed for it to become a true member of the family and perhaps to speak. It is essential that the second bird, too, be young when it joins your household if it is to adjust perfectly to its partner and fit in with humans and its new surroundings. This second bird, too, should gently be introduced to humans alone for the first week or two. This means that you need a second cage for this period. If you are reluctant to spend the money for one you can probably borrow one. It is best to keep the newcomer in a separate room before the two birds have a chance to get acquainted. And getting acquainted should be a gradual process. Bring the cage with the new bird into the room where the first one lives and leave it to the latter to discover the newcomer and initiate contact across the bars of the cage.

There may be "love at first sight," but disinterest or some aggression are equally likely. Depending on the behavior of the birds, you have to decide whether to continue separate housing for a while or whether to open both cages and let the birds deal with each other. If they are a true pair, i.e., a male and a female, problems are unlikely, because nature prescribes that the female be the dominant one and the male be content to let her have her way (see page 125). But if you have two birds of the same sex it may take a while to settle which bird takes the role of the male and which that of the female. During this phase some conflicts may arise between the two, but they rarely lead to real fights. But if a third parakeet that belongs to the opposite sex is introduced, there can develop violent battles of rivalry that call for human intervention. The contestants have to be separated. If two birds refuse to get along together and one even tries, perhaps, to mutilate the hated one when flying free in the room, you have no choice but to introduce separate flying hours. The "prisoner" is likely to protest loudly and express its outrage at this "unjust treatment" through amazing acrobatic contortions executed while hanging from the bars both upside down and right side up.

The Importance of Cleanliness

Personal hygiene takes up a major part of a bird's time, because only a bird with perfect plumage is fast and agile enough to outfly enemies. A parakeet, too, spends many hours a day preening itself. Though he does other things too, almost every "free moment" is devoted to preening. With great skill the long tail and wing feathers are pulled through the bill to remove every bit of dust or dirt. The small feathers are carefully pecked and smoothed. Feet and toes, too, are worked over with the bill. Every so often the head is rubbed over the oil gland above the base of the tail to grease the head feathers, and some fat is picked up in the bill, which is then evenly spread over the rest of the plumage. This thin oily layer on the feathers makes them water-repellent and prevents the bird from getting drenched in the rain and thus unable to fly. For cleaning the head feathers the bird has to resort to its toes while cleverly keeping its balance on one foot. If two parakeets live together they assist each other in preening the head, although the male will often scratch the female's head in a gesture of pure affection (see illustration on page 12).

In the wild, parakeets bathe only irregularly when they come across some open water for a quick drink. Generally only the belly feathers get wet. Ordinarily the morning dew serves as a shower as the birds move through the damp grass of the Australian steppe. Parakeets in captivity often enjoy lukewarm baths in the bath house, get wet under a dripping faucet, or like to be sprayed from a spray bottle.

Two parakeet males on a climbing tree. Displaying his acrobatic climbing skills, one of the birds, hanging head down, nibbles on the much loved spray millet. ▷

Keeping and Caring for Parakeets

Cleaning Chores

The parakeet's efforts at keeping clean have to be supplemented by its keeper because in captivity the bird is forced to live in such a tiny area. Cage, bird tree, and all other objects the bird uses or touches have to be kept meticulously clean if your pet is to remain free of pests and parasites and other harmful influences.

• Every day all the bird's dishes have to be rinsed with boiling water and dried thoroughly before they are filled again with fresh food and water. With a spoon reserved for this purpose remove all droppings and dirt from the bird gravel in the tray and add some fresh gravel. By doing this you prevent poisoning from contaminated food, skin diseases caused by contact with droppings, and ingestion of unhealthy dirt particles with the gravel. Dirty perches and branches are scrubbed with a small metal brush or an old toothbrush and cleaned with a cloth dampened with hot water.

• Once a week the bottom pan, which holds the tray, is washed with hot water.

• Twice a week the tray is completely emptied, washed with hot water, dried, and filled with clean gravel. (If two birds spend all their time in a cage the gravel should be replaced every other day.) Dirty perches and other objects are scrubbed and rinsed with hot water, and dried.

• Once a month the entire empty cage is moved to the bathtub or some other big tub. The bars and perches are first scrubbed under hot water and then the entire structure is hosed down with hot water and dried well. Branches and perches are sprayed with a mite spray after being mounted. Natural branches should be replaced every six to eight weeks.

Important: Hot water is the best thing for cleaning the cage and everything else a bird uses. Cleansers and chemical rinses are harmful and possibly even fatal for parakeets.

Gravel—As Litter and as an Aid to Digestion

The gravel you sprinkle on the bottom of the cage not only serves a hygienic purpose but is also important for the health of the bird. It will pick up a little gravel every day to help the digestion. Special bird gravel and oyster shell mixes also supply calcium and other minerals. Don't let yourself be tempted to line the cage floor with a kind of sandpaper, the so-called "bird carpet." The sand on this "carpet" is devoid of nutrients, and in the process of trying to peck off some sand, the parakeet is likely to swallow bits of the carpet's underside, which is harmful; some parakeets have died of this.

A clever parakeet can escape by squeezing through the slit in the bottom pan of the cage while you clean the gravel tray. If doors and windows are shut this is not serious. But if it is essential that the bird not

◁ Wild plants you can gather for your parakeet (the parts to be fed are in parentheses).
Above left: Cow vetch *Vicia cracca* (leaves and blossoms). Above right: Blue grass, *Poa chaixii* (seed heads). Middle left: Coltsfoot, *Tussilaga farfara* (flowers, half-ripe and ripe seeds). Middle right: Common dandelion, *Taraxacum officinale* (young leaves and half-ripe seeds). Below left: Common plaintain, *Plantago major* (seed heads). Below right: Common chickweed, *Stellaria media* (flowers, leaves, seeds).

39

get out of the cage, close off the slit with a cloth pinned to the bars with two clothespins or move the cage against the wall or a piece of furniture in such a way that the opening is blocked.

The Greatest Danger: Flying Away

A parakeet that is locked up all the time is a miserably bored creature, whereas one that is allowed to spend all day, or at least most of it, on its bird tree in the open room leads as ideal a life as possible for a bird in captivity. But the more lively and enterprising a bird is, the more dangers lurk in a room designed for human living (see List of Dangers on page 42).

But flying away is by far the greatest danger. A parakeet is a nimble acrobat and, like a snake, manages to fit through even the tiniest openings. A nomad by instinct, a parakeet has no need for the inborn ability to orient itself by landmarks or other visual stimuli. Living wild in Australia with always the flock to follow as the birds roam across the interior of the continent, parakeets have no permanent homes or territories (see page 108). A parakeet that escapes from its owner's home therefore has no ability to find its way back. The farther it gets from its familiar surroundings the greater its panic and the faster it flies. Most birds perish miserably after they fly from home, unless someone finds them by chance. And there are many opportunities of escape for a parakeet:

- Doors and windows that are left open.
- Scrabbling out of the cage while the gravel tray is out.
- A cage door that does not shut properly or that the bird has learned to open.
- Bars on the cage that are loose or bent so that the bird can squeeze through between them.
- The bird has a habit of sitting on its keeper's head or shoulder and is carried out into the open absentmindedly.
- A visitor can inadvertently carry it out. And a bird can fly off, especially out of fright.

Many owners of parakeets think that their bird cannot get out through a window hidden behind curtains or venetian blinds. But parakeets like to climb up on the slats, find even the tiniest opening, and climb down the other side. From there a bird is likely to take off for the wide world within a few minutes. All windows should therefore have screens. A light wood frame, the size of the window opening, covered with regular window screening or 3/8-inch hardware cloth can be mounted on the outside of the window. Then the room can be aired without danger of the bird escaping. Even a totally tame parakeet that has always stayed close to its human companion—near open windows, on the balcony, when taking out the garbage, on the way to the car—may after years of no incidents be frightened by a sudden bang, fly up in panic, and disappear. The bird will not be able to find its way back.

Everything else that threatens the safety of a parakeet in our care is mentioned in the List of Dangers starting on page 42, a list you should study carefully.

If you wonder whether you will be able to protect your parakeets from all these dangers, you might consider whether your birds would not be more safely housed in an indoor aviary (see page 23). But if you choose this option the aviary has to be large enough to give the birds ample room for

Keeping and Caring for Parakeets

flying. It also has to be completely bird-proof and allow for easy cleaning down to the farthest corner. To be sure, two parakeets living in an aviary will in time lose some of their attachment to their keeper; they gradually become more absorbed in each other, which will probably lead to mating and the production of offspring. It goes without saying that an aviary is out of the question for a single parakeet, because such a bird desperately needs close contact with humans.

A home-built indoor aviary that is spacious enough for several pairs of parakeets. It is equipped with climbing and sitting trees, objects to keep the birds occupied, and nest boxes. For grating it is best to use hardware cloth with the wires not more than ½ inch (12 mm) apart.

List of Dangers

Source of danger	Effects	Precautions
Bathroom	Drowning by slipping into the open toilet bowl or filled basin or bathtub. Poisoning through cleansers or chemicals.	Keep bird out. Never leave door open.
Bookshelves	Heart attack caused by fear if bird gets stuck behind books and can't get out without help.	Shove books directly against back wall or leave spaces between them. (Lay a couple of books sideways to prop up the others.)
Cage grating	Escaping if bars are too far apart or if there are holes in mesh. Getting head stuck (serious wounds) or strangling if spacing is wrong. Poisoning from rusty wires. Head and toe injuries from wire that is too thin and sharp.	Spacing between wires should always be ½″ (12 mm). Check frequently for rust and holes. Use hardware cloth.
Electric wires, outlets	Electrocution if wires are chewed.	Eliminate frayed or exposed wires. Unplug wires if bird is left unattended. Cover outlets with safety plugs.
String and yarn	Strangling in loops.	Don't leave string around.
Floors	Broken legs, bruised chest from landing too hard if obese or molting bird cannot fly properly.	Keep birds out of rooms with hard uncarpeted floors.
Curtains and drapes	Catching toes in loose weave; breaking legs in trying to get free. Poisoning from chewing on lead weights.	Curtains or drapes of close-weave material and without lead weights.
Containers with water (pans, vases, buckets)	Slipping in and drowning.	Cover containers. Don't let bird fly free while you are cleaning house.
Knitted and crocheted items	Catching toes, strangling.	Don't leave your knitting lying around; remove crocheted covers and pillows.

List of Dangers

Source of danger	Effects	Precautions
Toxic substances	Poisoning. Lead, verdigris, nicotine, rust, Teflon-coated pans, all kinds of cleansers and pesticides, and mercury are deadly; pencil tips, fillers for ball-point pens, alcohol, coffee, and pungent spices are harmful.	Keep all toxic items and substances out of the bird's reach. (Watch out for lead especially).
Windows, glass walls	Flying against glass and sustaining concussion, fractured skull, or broken neck.	Hang curtains in front of windows, glass doors, etc., and train bird to recognize transparent barrier (see page 29).
Stove tops	Burns, burning to death if bird lands on hot burner.	Don't let bird loose in kitchen. Put covered pot of water on unused hot burner.
Candles	Burns.	Do without candlelight while bird is flying free.
Glues	Fatal poisoning caused by vapors from glue.	Keep all animals out of room where glue is used (for repair and crafts). Air room thoroughly afterwards.
Kitchen	Birds can suffocate in steam and vapors; heat from cooking, as well as necessary airing, can cause colds and other illnesses.	Keep bird out of kitchen, or air kitchen frequently. Keep bird out of drafts.
Human feet	Being stepped on.	Watch out, and always remember that there might be a bird underfoot.
Human food	Bad for the bird's health. Minute bits of white bread, dry cake, and a grain of salt (if bird shows craving) are permissible occasionally.	Avoid feeding human food; don't let the bird pilfer.
Wastebaskets	Sliding in, starving, heart attack from fear if basket is smooth inside and bird cannot get out.	Use woven baskets or line with wire mesh.

List of Dangers

Source of danger	Effects	Precautions
Plants	Poisoning, often fatal, from plants like daffodil, mistletoe, yew, hyacinth, narcissus, oleander, primroses, wax plant (*Hoya carnosa*), nux vomica, periwinkle (*Vinca minor*), all Dieffenbachia species, and all plants of the nightshade family. A cactus can cause extremely serious wounds if a bird lands on one.	Forego poisonous plants in the bird's room. Kangaroo vine (cissus), hibiscus, and ferns are nonpoisonous.
Cupboards and drawers	Starving to death or suffocating if the bird is locked in and its plight goes unnoticed.	Nosy parakeets like to investigate drawers and cupboards and females look for nesting possibilities there. Always check carefully before closing.
Pots and bowls	Drowning in liquid contents; scalding if liquid is hot. Birds regard food and whipped liquids as landing sites.	Cover containers; keep bird out of kitchen. Don't let bird fly free during meals.
Seats	Being squashed by people sitting down.	Make sure there is no bird under you before sitting down.
Perches	Uneven distribution of weight, insufficient muscle development, cartilage formation, overgrowth of claws if perches are too thin. Fractures and other injuries if perches are not mounted securely; falling perches can hit birds.	Use proper perches of different thicknesses. Mount them securely.
Sun	Sunstroke or heart attack if the sun is too strong.	Bird can be exposed to sun but must be able to retreat to shade.
Cracks between furniture and walls	Sliding down, getting stuck. If the bird cannot free itself it may die of fright.	Plug cracks with wood or cardboard.
Pointed objects	Injuries, deep puncture wounds.	Don't leave sharp objects lying around; keep out of bird's reach.

List of Dangers

Source of danger	Effects	Precautions
Temperature fluctuations	Colds if temperature drops suddenly; heatstroke or heart attack in great or sudden heat.	Avoid rapid temperature changes; gradually acclimate bird to new temperature. (Room temperatures between 75° and 50° F (24°–10° C) are acceptable.
Doors	Getting caught and squashed if door is shut quickly; escaping; sickness caused by drafts from open doors.	Care in opening and closing doors helps prevent these dangers.
Pests	Internal and external parasites can cause diseases.	Do all cleaning chores regularly and thoroughly. Treat bird promptly if it is infested; disinfect cage, toys, favorite perches, but never spray or dust bird (danger of suffocation or poisoning); use at most a powder directly on bird.
Wash basins, tubs	Slipping, drowning; birds may try to land on suds.	Keep bird out of bathroom; don't let it fly free while you do dishes.
Detergents, cleansers, chemicals	Poisoning if bird absorbs any of these.	Keep all household cleansers in closed cupboards; carefully rinse off all traces after use.
Vases, pitchers, glasses, etc.	Sliding in and—if bird cannot get out again—suffocating, starving to death, or heart attack from panic.	Fill empty vessels with bird gravel or crumpled paper, or cover vessels; store empty glasses upside down.
Cigarettes	Smoke-filled air is harmful and nicotine is deadly.	It is best not to smoke near bird; if someone does smoke, ventilate room regularly (avoid drafts). Never let parakeet nibble on a cigarette.
Drafts	Colds, crop inflammation, pneumonia; parakeets are extremely sensitive to even momentary drafts.	Avoid drafts at all cost. Check with a burning candle; the flame shows the slightest draft that a person hardly feels but that harms a bird.

The Parakeet's Diet

A Balanced Diet

To stay healthy over the years parakeets need adequate opportunity for climbing and flying, plenty of light and fresh air, and a well-balanced and varied diet. In their native Australia parakeets live primarily on the half-ripe and fully ripe seeds of many grasses (see page 118). During the mating periods plenty of half-ripe seeds—which are especially nutritious—are available to meet the dietary needs of the nestlings.

When the birds cross dry areas in their constant quest for food, they find only dry seeds and have to have drinking water to be able to soften these in their crops. But since most rivers and water holes in their range are usually dried up because of the long dry season, the parakeets move through the damp steppe in the early morning, drinking the dew drops.

It has been shown that parakeets pick up some sand and tiny stones off the ground along with the seeds as an aid to digestion. They also eat fresh greens, but we don't know if their diet occasionally includes insects and their larvae and eggs. This may not seem like much of a menu; nevertheless parakeets in the wild always eat fresh seeds that contain all essential nutrients. The parakeets we keep in cages, on the other hand, have to take what we give them. A conscientious aviculturist will always choose the bird's primary food—a mixture of birdseed—with special care. This means among other things that the birds are given no old birdseed, for seeds that have been stored too long no longer contain all the nutrients birds need to stay healthy.

The Basic Staple: Mixed Birdseed

Experts recommend feeding parakeets a seed mixture consisting mainly of canary grass seeds and several varieties of millet, to which oats, niger seed, and linseed are added. Unmixed seeds can sometimes be found in pet stores and seed stores. But the diet of parakeets is commonly available in ready-to-use mixtures. Pet food companies compose and market balanced birdseed mixtures, often enriched with vitamins and minerals. Packaged birdseed mixture can, of course, be purchased not only at pet stores but also at supermarkets; always check the packing date stamped on the bag before buying it.

Food grains and seeds—for the use of humans as well as birds—are harvested once a year and, under proper storage, retain their viability until the next planting season. The vital substances keep about one year, though the nutritional value decreases gradually. But the seeds remain edible up to two years. Crucial for the food value of all grains and seeds is proper storage, namely, in dark but airy spaces. From the day that seeds intended as bird food are packaged they are no longer exposed to much air. That is why it is important to buy birdseed with as recent a packing date as possible, i.e., within four to five months. Even with this precaution it is advisable to take a spoonful of seeds from any bag of commercial birdseed and test its viability. (Instructions for sprouting seeds are on page 49.) As long as seeds sprout they still have the vital substances that bring alive the new plant that lies dormant within the seed and thus also supply the birds with the essential nutrients. If in your seed test only a small

Forage Plants to Gather Wild or to Grow

Annual bluegrass
Poa annua
(True grasses)
2 to 12 inches (5-30 cm) tall; forms lawns. Found in meadows, fields, waste places, gardens. Plant in May; use seeds of wild plants. Harvest from April to October. Feed half-ripe and ripe seeds (can also be frozen).

Cow vetch
Vicia cracca
(Pea family)
Up to 20 inches (50 cm) tall; with reddish blue flowers. Found in **meadows**, among bushes, in woods and gardens. Plant in March; use seeds of wild plants. Harvest from May to September. Feed leaves and flowers (high in protein).

Finger grass
Panicum sanguinale
(True grasses)
4 to 24 inches (10-60 cm) tall; plant spreads on ground; seed stalks rise up straight. Found in woods, cultivated fields, fallow land, gardens. Plant in March; use seeds of wild plants. Harvest from July to September. Feed half-ripe and ripe seeds (can also be frozen).

English daisy
Bellis perennis
(Composite family)
Up to 5 inches (15 cm) tall, grows in lawns, with white to pink flowers. Found in meadows, along fields, in yards and lawns. Plant in March; use seeds of wild plants or, for cultivated strains, seeds from seed houses. Harvest from May to June. Feed half-ripe and ripe seeds (flowers past blooming with stems removed).

Field pansy
Viola tricolor
(Violet family)
2 to 10 inches (5-25 cm) tall; four wild species and many cultivated strains. Found in meadows, fallow land, gardens. Plant in September; use seeds of wild plants or, for cultivated strains, seeds from seed houses. Harvest from April to June. Feed opened seed capsules.

Shepherd's purse
Capsella bursa-pastoris
(Mustard family)
Up to 16 inches (40 cm) tall, with white flowers. Found in cultivated fields, along paths, on fallow land, and in gardens. Plant in October or November; use seeds of wild plants. Harvest from May to October. Feed entire plant; give in small bunches.

Dog rose
Rosa canina
(Rose family)
Medium-sized bushes with dark pink flowers; fruits (rose hips) bright red. Found along paths, railroad embankments, edges of woods, in gardens. Plant in the fall; get root stock from nurseries (also for cultivated forms). Harvest from September to November. Feed rose hips (can also be frozen).

Hawthorns
Crataegus
(Upright thorny plants)
Medium-sized bush with white flowers; fruits bright red. Found on rocky slopes, edges of fields and woods. Plant in October or November; get root stock from nurseries. Harvest from May to June (flowers) and September to October (fruits). Feed flowers and fruit; you can also give entire branches.

47

portion sprouts, the mixture has been stored too long or is otherwise damaged and therefore practically worthless. The seeds should not only be viable but also show no sign of rot or mildew and be free of vermin. You can smell rot; mildew is visible; and vermin show up in seeds that are clumped together and have cobweblike filaments emanating from these clumps.

Check the basic food of your parakeet constantly and be sure to keep it not in a plastic bag or container but in a cloth bag hung in an airy, dark spot. Birdseed can be left in a cardboard box but should also be kept in a dry and dark place.

You can buy parakeet treats in the shape of sticks, little hearts, or rings. These are made of the normal seeds parakeets eat but with a bit of honey or sugar syrup added so that the seeds will stick to the shaped base. Since pecking the seeds off this base gives the parakeet a chance to use its bill, these treats are often popular with the birds. Whether the parakeets really enjoy the treats as food is unclear. Birds that are bored and pass the time picking at these treats may consume too many calories and get too fat, but this pecking is often the only distraction available to parakeets that are bored because they are hardly ever allowed out of the cage and usually get too little attention from people.

Fruit and Vegetables

In addition to its basic food a parakeet needs fresh fruit and greens every day. Don't be discouraged if your bird leaves much of this food untouched. Nobody can force a parakeet to eat anything. If not accustomed from its early days to fresh food, a parakeet will at first suspiciously avoid these unfamiliar things. If two or more parakeets live together, one of them will be more courageous than the others and at some point take a nibble of the fruit or greens. Then you can be sure that the others will follow suit. The birds are most likely to try some fresh herbs or greens, preferably chickweed, young dandelion leaves, or spinach. If you gather plants yourself, keep in mind that even thorough washing does not remove traces of exhaust fumes that can poison a bird. Be sure therefore to pick plants only far away from roads. Wash all greens several times in lukewarm water and let drip well (unless the leaves are to provide the "dew bath"). Never give a bird wilted greens or—worse—ones that smell bad.

There is another way to provide fresh, "unpoisoned" greens for your parakeet. Pet stores offer special "bird meadows." These are small pots with seeds sown in them (usually a mixture of plaintain, garden cress, lettuce, and grass seeds). The pots are equipped with special mountings for easy attachment to the bars of the cage.

Unless you can get organically grown lettuce it is better not to feed your parakeet lettuce leaves, because what you can ordinarily buy has not only been grown with insecticides but also treated against quick wilting. Residues of these poisons can kill a parakeet.

Fruit and vegetables, too, have to be carefully washed with lukewarm water and thoroughly dried before being given to parakeets. Root vegetables and fruit (especially citrus fruit) should even be peeled to get rid of all traces of insecticides. In time you will

The Parakeet's Diet

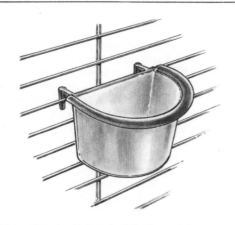

Dishes that can be hung on the bars of the cage are especially useful for supplementary foods like fruit and greens.

learn what your parakeet likes to eat and what it won't touch. Offer carrots at first in grated form; once used to the taste, your bird will probably come to enjoy gnawing on larger pieces of carrot stuck between the bars of the cage. Pieces of apple and pear can be served the same way. Cherries, strawberries, grapes, sections of tangerines, or slices of kiwi fruit can be given in a small bowl, but a tame parakeet will like best to pick them from the keeper's hand. Many parakeets like to peck the little seeds off strawberries before tasting the fruit itself. Grapes are usually cut in half before serving; the birds then like to drink the juice out of the grape halves or suck happily on the little "brushes" that are left on the stems when the grapes are pulled off.

Important: Plants and fruit like the ones mentioned are a vital part of a parakeet's diet, since some vitamins in them are either not present in the seed mixture, or are present only in minute amounts. Offer as many different fresh items as possible, and never lose your patience. But make sure your parakeet never gets spoiled or rotten fruit and vegetables and that fresh foods are removed after a few hours because of quick spoilage on hot days or in heated rooms. Food should be at room temperature, never straight from the refrigerator.

Sprouted Seeds

Parakeets need especially nutritious food during the molt and during the mating period. Sprouted seeds are rich in important vitamins and have the added advantage that most parakeets like sprouted seeds and eat them without hesitation. But sprouted seeds should be given not only at times of stress but also as a tonic in the winter and early spring when fruits and vegetables have lower vitamin content than in the summer. Sprouted seeds should definitely be offered if a parakeet is reluctant to eat fruit and vegetables.

You can sprout the seeds of your usual birdseed mixture but should also buy hulled oat and wheat kernels from a health food store for sprouting. As soon as viable kernels absorb water, a chemical reaction triggers the sprouting. In this process vitamins, minerals, and trace elements are unlocked, thus increasing the food value of soaked and, even more, of sprouted kernels.

Soak one teaspoon of your standard birdseed mixture in a little water. The seeds should be covered by about ¾ of an inch (2 cm) of water. After about 24 hours rinse the seeds with lukewarm water in a sieve and

49

The Parakeet's Diet

put them in a shallow bowl or glass. Cover them with a small plate to keep them from drying out and let them stand for another 24 to 48 hours. After 24 hours they are ready to be served as soaked kernels; after 48 hours, as sprouts. Rinse them once more under lukewarm water and let them drip well before serving. Important: Soaked and sprouted kernels spoil quickly. Serve them in the morning in a separate dish and after one or two hours remove what has not been consumed. This avoids the possibility of your bird getting sick from eating kernels that are beginning to rot. Gradually you will get to know just how much of this supplemental food your bird will eat per day.

Let the birds themselves determine how long to continue giving them the sprouts. When you first start the regimen they will rush at the sprouts eagerly every day, but gradually appetite for them subsides until the sprout dish is hardly touched. That's the time to skip sprouts for a few weeks. But parakeets also like unsprouted hulled oat kernels. You may add about a teaspoonful of them to a bird's basic birdseed mixture every day, assuming your parakeet is not too heavy or fat because of inadequate exercise. Natural food stores as well as most pet stores carry these oats. Grains have to be stored in cloth bags where air can circulate.

Important Supplements to the Diet

Spray millet is not only a parakeet's favorite treat, but also an especially nutritious, easily digested natural food that can be used to nurse sick and weak birds back to health. One whole spray per day provides the needed high energy to brooding birds and their offspring. But under ordinary circumstances you should serve spray millet sparingly, because parakeets put on weight—something to be avoided—when given too much. A healthy, not too fat parakeet may be given about two inches of a spray a day or, if the bird also gets oat kernels (sprouted or unsprouted), spray millet and oats on alternating days.

Once a week you may give your parakeet some supplemental protein in the form of one teaspoon of hard-boiled egg yolk mixed with some low-fat cottage cheese. If you coarsely grind grains for your own breakfast you can add some freshly cracked grains to the egg yolk and cottage cheese mixture.

Some pet stores sell imported mixtures of special seeds enriched with vitamins to be given in addition to the basic food. The claim that these special seeds enhance a bird's speaking talent has yet to be substantiated. But the seeds with their extra vitamins clearly benefit the birds. Another special seed mixture supplies needed nutrients during molt. There are other seeds, powders, and drops sold as supplements to the basic food, but in my opinion such supplements are not necessary if a parakeet's diet is carefully composed.

I do think it very important, however, to give vitamin supplements, because there is no way of checking the vitamin content of the basic seed mixture, fruit, and vegetables. If you cannot grow your parakeet's food yourself you have to feed seeds that may have been stored too long and produce that may not be fresh. It is a well-known fact that all nutrients, but especially vitamins, start to deteriorate—sometimes very quickly—after plants are harvested. But vitamins

The Parakeet's Diet

are crucial, and the smaller the organism, the more severely it will react to vitamin deficiency. That is why it is advisable to add vitamins to a parakeet's drinking water even if you provide varied fresh food, supplement it periodically with sprouts, and test the viability of the basic birdseed mixture.

You can buy vitamin supplements for birds at pet stores as well as at drug stores. The dosage depends on the size of the bird. Look at the expiration date on the package; vitamins that are too old are worthless.

Parakeets need not only all the vitamins but also calcium and phosphorus. Both these minerals are present only in small amounts in the foods thus far mentioned. To make up for this you should give your bird a good mineral stone for nibbling and sharpening its beak. Always keep a mineral stone in reserve, because sometimes a bird that hasn't touched the stone for weeks will suddenly go after it avidly and keep gnawing on it until it disintegrates. When you buy a mineral stone be sure to read the package. It should say something like: "Mineral stone containing all elements necessary for strengthening the skeleton and forming the feathers." Pet stores also have sepia shells, which are the calcium-rich internal shells of cuttlefish, but these are not suitable for gnawing, especially by female parakeets, because the salt in them can lead to egg binding. Calcium is also contained in the special bird gravel, which has crushed oyster shells added to it. The gravel on the bottom of the cage serves not only a hygienic purpose; birds also eat some of it to help them digest (see page 39), and in the process they absorb small particles of calcium.

The Amount of Food

How much food does a parakeet need a day? The answer is: That depends on the age, the habits, and the activities of the given bird. I cannot even indicate amounts in spoonfuls, because the food dish will be covered with a layer of empty seed hulls after the birds have eaten several times. Parakeets peel every kernel and let the hull drop back in the dish, and then they cannot find the kernels underneath the hulls. You therefore have to remove the hulls with a small spoon or blow them off the dish over the garbage pail. That is why you should put only about two teaspoons of seeds in the dish to start and add a little every time you remove the empty husks. An even better idea is to have two dishes with birdseed per bird or to resort to an automatic dispenser (see page 18).

Birds have an active metabolism and therefore need small amounts of food several times a day. Never leave a parakeet without food for any length of time. A well-adjusted, happy bird with enough to keep it occupied, freedom of movement, a chance to fly regularly, and human affection or a partner to keep it busy will not eat more than it needs. Only neglected, lonely parakeets overeat out of boredom and become overweight. It is easy to recognize when a parakeet starts getting too heavy; it flies awkwardly and pants at the slightest exertion. If you take such a bird in your hand you can barely feel the breastbone through the muscles and fat. If this is the case you have to act right away and eliminate all high-calorie supplementary food, especially spray millet, oat kernels, and the egg yolk and cottage cheese mixture. In-

The Parakeet's Diet

stead, plenty of fresh produce is added to the basic birdseed. Under no circumstance make a bird fast because it is too fat; simply cut down some on its daily portion of basic food. Obviously the best remedy for "fat from misery" in the case of a parakeet is to keep it occupied and to provide plenty of exercise.

Check every day to make sure that food and water dispensers function perfectly.

Also keep in mind that you might be unexpectedly prevented from coming home some day. Your parakeet should have enough birdseed and perhaps other supplementary food to survive for two or three days in such a case. Even stale water would be better under these circumstances than none at all.

Don't get angry if your parakeet invents all kinds of tricks to be able to peck seeds off the cage bottom or living room floor. That is the favorite way of eating for a bird who in nature finds its food on the ground (see page 118).

The Drinking Water

All cage birds need fresh drinking water every day. Normally they are given tap water that has sat for a while and is not too cold. If you want to do better than that you can substitute a special, commercially available bird drink. Even better than that is bottled, uncarbonated mineral water that lists the mineral contents. The drinking water is boiled or replaced by a light tea only for certain disorders (see page 69).

Health Care and Parakeet Diseases

Most keepers of parakeets think of their birds as part of the family and are as concerned about their pets' health as about that of other family members. In recent times biologists and nature filmmakers have recognized parakeets as interesting birds of many talents and have devoted serious study to parakeets living wild in Australia (see page 106) as well as to their cousins bred in captivity (see page 136).

The parakeet's popularity with humans has had some serious negative effects on the breed. As in the case of many other animals that reproduce relatively easily in captivity, a subjective human standard was developed of the "ideal" parakeet. The breeder's aim here is not to produce a bird as similar as possible to the one living in the wild; instead, color of plumage, standardized notions of shape, and, last but not least, quantitative breeding results usually take precedence. In addition, too often the necessary care for healthy development is neglected, and the birds' health suffers from inadequate housing, one-sided diet, lack of exercise, and questionable methods of transportation. The result of all this is magnificent-looking parakeets that are, however, predisposed to serious diseases even when young. Sometimes months or even several years pass without any sign of such a weakness in the parakeet's looks or behavior. But suddenly the bird is sick and the owner has no idea what accounts for this change. The owner seldom finds the cause or even a plausible explanation. On the other hand I want to stress that although breeding methods and conditions may be the cause of illness, we should never use this excuse to cover up our own negligence.

If you raise parakeets yourself, please never forget: The better the conditions under which the breeding birds are kept and the fewer the strain crossings that might negatively affect the bird's vitality, the healthier and hardier the offspring will be.

An Ounce of Prevention

Many diseases can be avoided if parakeets are kept properly, and a bird in top physical condition is more likely to survive if an illness does strike. Be sure, therefore, to commit to memory the following condensed list of what is good for birds and what is bad for them.

What a parakeet needs:
• A varied diet in adequate amounts.
• Fruit and vegetables that are fresh and not chemically treated.
• Birdseed that is not spoiled and has not been stored too long.
• Drinking water, uncarbonated mineral water, or "bird drink" (from a pet store) that is served clean, fresh, and not too cold.
• Natural branches—frequently replaced by new ones—from unsprayed fruit trees or other nonpoisonous trees growing far from roads with heavy traffic. The branches should be of different thicknesses for healthy foot exercise and for gnawing.
• Adequate daily opportunity for flying and moving around outside the cage in well-aired rooms.
• Strict cleanliness of all items a bird touches.
• Parakeets kept singly need several not too short periods a day during which their human partner gives them full attention; regular playtimes and physical closeness, includ-

ing whistling, singing, and talking with the bird are essential.

What is harmful to a bird:
● Sudden temperature fluctuations (moving from a heated room to an unheated one); summer travel in a hot car. Any draft, even in warm weather.
● Food that is rotting, otherwise spoiled, or treated with chemicals.
● All food intended for humans, especially food that is salty, strongly spiced or sweetened, or has a high fat content; alcohol.
● Unsuitable or poisonous indoor plants (see List of Dangers starting on page 42).
● Exposure to direct sunshine if there is no shady retreat.
● Musty rooms; tobacco smoke or other smoke; toxic or caustic fumes; penetrating smells.
● Sitting alone in a cage for hours on end and being bored and lonely.

Always keep a vigilant eye on your healthy parakeet and be familiar with its habits, likes and dislikes, favorite treats, and general behavior, so that you will notice any change right away. But don't be overly anxious. Despite the parakeet's pronounced liking for routine, a favorite old habit may be abandoned overnight; the fruit that he craved up to now, for instance, is suddenly rejected. Weather, changes in temperature, loneliness, or a temporary cutting back of time spent with the bird can cause short-term changes in behavior and vital functions that do not signal an acute illness. Many parakeets react with slight diarrhea not only to too cool a bath but also to insufficient attention, unfamiliar surroundings, or fright. The diarrhea will disappear after a couple of hours.

Symptoms of Disease

There is reason for serious worry if the bird acts sick for several hours or entire days. A parakeet that does not feel well looks listless, withdraws from its partner, fluffs up the feathers slightly, turns its head 180°, and tucks its beak into its back feathers. Such a bird stands on both legs and isn't really asleep but looks with dull eyes at nothing in particular. A healthy parakeet sleeps in the same posture (see page 132) but with one leg pulled up and tucked into the belly feathers. Of course there are exceptions: Many healthy birds, too, rest on both legs when sleeping.

A sick parakeet will stir around in the food dish with its bill but hardly eat any seeds. Often the bird will seem exceptionally thirsty. If two parakeets live together you sometimes see the healthy partner preen the sick one more than usual.

If the bird gets worse it weakly lies on its perch or the bottom of the cage in an almost horizontal position. The tail feathers droop down from the perch instead of sticking out straight and continuing the line of the back as they do in a healthy bird. If the bird is in pain it will now and then raise itself up with feet wide apart on the perch, make itself

Parakeets spend many hours a day grooming their ▷ plumage. Above left: The tail feathers are pulled through the bill. Above right: Some oil is taken from the uropygial gland at the base of the tail and spread over the plumage. Below left: The female on the left is carefully smoothing the little feathers over her mate's eyes. Below right: The male is asking the female to scratch his throat.

Health Care and Parakeet Diseases

thin as in fear, and stick the folded wings out sideways. Often it will bite in the air several times in succession. When the respiratory system is affected, the bird's rattling or whistling breathing is sometimes audible.

Other important signs for alarm are changes in the droppings and perhaps slime discharged from the crop. If the droppings remain watery or—worse—slimy or with a reddish or greenish discoloration, they should be analyzed as soon as possible for bacteria and parasites. A slimy discharge from the crop suggests an inflammation of the crop that should be treated immediately.

Don't be frightened, on the other hand, if you find your parakeet busily feeding its live partner, a plastic imitation, or even its mirror image with kernels it is choking up. Female parakeets satisfy their instinctive need to raise nestlings with this surrogate activity, and lonely male birds feed their mirror image as an act of love for what they think of as their mate.

An occasional "sneezing" does not mean that your bird has a cold. Sneezing, or what sounds like it, cleans out the mucous nasal membranes. If birds "yawn," which they do quite often, this is an attempt to make up for a lack of oxygen; when this happens see to it that the room gets additional fresh air.

◁ Display feeding. Above and below: In the course of courtship display the male repeatedly feeds the female to bring her into breeding condition. Actual food is not always passed to the other bird in the course of display feeding.

The Molt

A bird is not sick when it molts, but it is more sensitive to unfavorable conditions during this time. The molt is a natural process, during which all birds replace their feathers. The seasons and the frequency of molt depend on the life rhythm of the particular species. Most songbirds molt after the last mating period of the year; migratory birds molt in good time before the long journey to winter quarters. Birds that depend on the color of their plumage for camouflage may grow new feathers as often as three times a year, while large birds, such as eagles and cranes, molt only every other year.

The juvenile plumage of a parakeet is very similar to that of a mature bird, except that the juvenile colors are somewhat paler. The typical wavy pattern extends from the back of the head across the forehead down to the ceres (the swellings at the base of the nostrils). At about three months of age the young birds enter their first molt, and after that it is impossible to tell them from their parents. Parakeets living wild have no set molting seasons, because their life rhythm is entirely determined by the climatic conditions of the regions they inhabit in Australia. These birds temporarily abandon their nomadic way of life only when they find areas where plentiful rainfalls promise abundant vegetation for some time to come. Such an opportunity is used for mating and sometimes for raising several broods. Water and food are then available close by and there is no need for long flights, so the birds start a "gentle" molt at the same time. Parakeets in the wild never replace all their feathers in a molt; such a curtailment of their flying ability would be too risky. Our parakeets raised in captivity therefore have some difficulty establishing a reasonable rhythm for molting. Many birds start their molt when the central heating season starts. Some molt in the spring or the middle of the summer, and others shed relatively few feathers at a time at several points of the year without any recognizable reason for the timing. But stressful experiences, such as transport, change of surroundings, or being caught can also trigger a molt. Young and healthy birds undergo molt with barely any sign of impairment. You may see them pecking at their plumage more than usual to pull out loose feathers or remove a thin layer of substance enveloping the new feathers growing in. This substance then floats to the bottom of the cage in tiny flakes. Older or not altogether healthy birds, on the other hand, can be so weakened by the molt as to be unable to fly. Here you have to watch carefully. The bird might be unable to fly up from the floor or reach its cage and will then need your help.

It would be altogether wrong and cruel to interfere with the process of molting by trying to pull out feathers that seem to be loose. Only the bird itself can feel which feathers are ready to come out. Pulling them out by force is painful, may cause bleeding, and injures the papillae in the dermis that play an important part in the growth of the new feathers. The long tail feathers take about two months to grow in, the big primaries about four to six weeks, and the small feathers, including those with the throat spots, about three weeks. Weak birds or poorly nourished ones sometimes suffer from arrested molt, i.e., the new feathers grow in reluctantly and tend to be stunted or defective.

In any case parakeets should be protected from temperature fluctuations, all drafts, and frightening experiences during the molt. They need constant warmth, proper air humidity, quiet, and a diet—including sprouted kernels, fresh greens, and fruit— that is rich in vitamins and minerals. Calcium and vitamin supplements are also very important.

If the bird does not seem up to par or looks sick it should be exposed to infrared light (see page 61) for five to ten minutes a day. A bird that is not timid or easily startled can be sprayed with lukewarm water every other day while it molts. (Be sure the spray bottle you use has never been in contact with any pesticides.)

Molting from Fright

This form of molt is rare in pet birds. (To a parakeet living wild it offers a possible chance of escaping an enemy.) The sudden fright of being caught clumsily can cause a bird to lose a whole bunch of feathers. If this has happened to your parakeet, treat it with special loving care for a few days, protecting it from further unhappy experiences of this kind, and otherwise treat the bird as though it were undergoing a real molt.

French Molt

The French molt is an abnormal development that used to be considered a result of hereditary factors or inadequate nutrition during the nestling period. According to the most recent findings it seems

Health Care and Parakeet Diseases

likely that this condition is caused by a virus. Birds suffering from French molt are called runners or hoppers because at about four weeks their large wing feathers that have just grown in fall out or break off. Either they don't grow again at all, or if they do they fall out again before they are large enough for flying.

A parakeet wing with normal feathers.

Parakeets suffering from French molt lose their primaries as nestlings and remain unable to fly for the rest of their lives.

These birds are usually permanently unable to fly and should therefore be kept in very large cages—with plenty of natural branches—where they have lots of opportunity for climbing and gnawing. Never let such birds breed, and avoid contact between them and healthy birds, because the virus is contagious.

Minor Problems

Superficial injuries, overgrown claws, and excessive growth of the beak are not, properly speaking, diseases. But if these conditions are left unattended, sickness or injuries can result.

Superficial Injuries

An irate female parakeet is capable of inflicting serious wounds on a rival in a contest over a nesting place or out of sheer jealousy; on rare occasions males, too, fight bitterly enough to leave visible traces. Then there is the danger that a bird might injure itself on some worn wire on the cage or on sharp or pointed objects. Bleeding wounds or ones with scabs on them—usually on the feet, more rarely under the feathers—require no medical treatment. Simply dab the injured place or dirtied feathers with boiled, strained, lukewarm chamomile tea. If a wound is still bleeding, press coagulant cotton against it for a while. A special healing salve for birds (available at pet stores) speeds the healing process. Take the bird to a veterinarian only if there is considerable loss of blood or if the bleeding does not stop. In that case a blood vessel might be damaged.

Overgrown Claws

In older and frail birds the toenails sometimes grow excessively long, in extreme cases even curling like a corkscrew. The usual explanation is that the claws do not get enough wear on artificial perches that are smooth and too thin and do not allow for enough exercise. I am skeptical about this explanation because I have seen and know many parakeets that are not confined to a cage, perch only on natural branches, have complete freedom of movement, have rough stones in their living area, and still develop overgrown toenails. It is true, of course, that no caged bird can be provided with enough opportunity to wear down its claws sufficiently. Nevertheless, accelerated growth of the claws usually goes hand in hand with some weakness. A bird with claws that grow too long needs steady care and high-quality food and should be watched closely. Since claws that are too long hamper and endanger a bird (catching in textiles or in a chain, getting stuck in cracks, imped-

This is the proper way to hold a parakeet to clip its claws. Be careful not to cut into the quick and try not to have the claw splinter (inset).

ing grooming) the toenails have to be cut periodically with nail scissors.

For this procedure, as well as for any other treatment, the bird has to be caught and held properly. Don't try to catch a bird in flight; you could easily injure its wings or shoulder joints. Also avoid needlessly chasing your parakeet back and forth in its cage; this would scare the bird half to death. If all else fails, darken the room and reach for the bird from above while talking soothingly. Hold it loosely but properly in your hand: The bird's back should be in the palm of your hand with its head between your thumb and forefinger, your middle finger encircling its abdomen, and the toe about to be treated being held gently but firmly between your ring finger and little finger. Don't turn the bird upside down so that it lies on its back. Now hold the toe up to a bright light so that you can clearly see the dark blood vessels in the horny tissue of the claw. Trim the overgrown claw close to the end of the vein, cutting at an angle to leave the upper and outer tip longer than the inner part of the nail (see illustration on left). If you should nick the vein a drop of blood will form but it causes hardly any pain to the bird. If the cut continues to bleed press styptic cotton against the end of the claw until the bleeding stops. Timid bird owners can ask a bird breeder, pet dealer, or avian veterinarian for help with this chore. Some pet stores offer free claw and bill trimming to their customers.

Excessive Growth of the Beak

Periodically thin splinters will chip off the tip of a parakeet's beak. This is a normal part of the renewal of the beak's tissue. But

Health Care and Parakeet Diseases

in older parakeets, for reasons as yet unknown, the beak sometimes grows too fast in spite of frequent whetting. Usually only the upper mandible is affected, but more rarely the upper and lower mandibles cross each other because they both grow too long simultaneously. In either case the bird is hampered in its intake of food. If nothing were done to help, eating would eventually become impossible, and the excessively long beak would injure the skin of the crop region. Don't let things get that far. The best thing to do is to take the bird to an experienced avian veterinarian, breeder, or pet dealer to have the beak trimmed with proper (nail) clippers. If the bird has a predisposition for excessive beak growth, regular trimming may be necessary, sometimes as often as every four weeks. Competent bird owners can quickly learn to perform this duty themselves and dispense with the trips to the veterinarian. If in spite of all your caution the trimming should result in minor bleeding, apply styptic cotton to the beak until the blood stops. If the beak is very brittle, dab it with slightly warmed glycerine or olive oil before wielding the clippers.

First Aid

If one day you notice that your parakeet or one of several birds looks sick, is injured, or is in some other way disabled, you have to act immediately and perhaps apply first aid. To be ready for first aid without loss of time you should have the following items ready at all times:
- tweezers
- eye dropper
- blunt scissors
- iodine
- styptic cotton
- charcoal
- salve for burns
- healing salve
- narrow bandages
- infrared lamp

If you keep more than one bird a small "hospital cage" to isolate a sick bird from the healthy ones prevents disease from spreading to other birds, guarantees peace and quiet to the sick bird, and makes it possible to supply uniform heat if necessary and to administer accurate doses of medications in the drinking water or food.

An obviously sick bird is best quartered in a warm, quiet room without bright lights or direct sunshine. Line the bottom of the cage with a double layer of absorbent paper and supply some gravel in a special dish. This is the only way to check the consistency of the excreta, for in case of serious sickness the veterinarian has to be able to examine and possibly analyze a sample of the droppings free of gravel. Many pet dealers are very knowledgeable about parakeets so that you can ask for advice at a good pet store if your parakeet is sick.

Infrared Radiation Therapy

The first thing to do if your bird looks sick is to treat it with infrared light. Place a lamp with an infrared bulb of 150 to 250 watts about 8 to 12 inches (20–30 cm) from the cage in such a way that only half of the cage is exposed to the light. This gives the bird a chance to choose the temperature that suits it. Turn the light on for thirty minutes three times a day. If the bird seems obviously better with the light on, you can leave the lamp on, but check the temperature in the cage and make sure it does not rise above 95° F (35° C). Infrared rays give off warmth that penetrates under the skin and stimulates circulation and metabolism. The blood vessels expand and waste products are eliminated more quickly. The rays also activate the immune system of the bird. Often a bird will perk up after the first exposure to infrared light. When the lamp is turned off the temperature in the cage should not drop too rapidly. The best procedure is to gradually move the lamp away from the cage and then to shine a regular 60-watt bulb on the cage. Shade the bulb to dim the light.

If you hear wheezing or rattling noises when your bird breathes, if it produces slime from the crop or from the nostrils, clearly gasps for air, or hangs from the bars of the cage by the beak in an effort to breathe more freely through a stretched trachea, you can be practically certain that the bird is suffering from a respiratory ailment. The bird will need not only infrared radiation but also high air humidity. Place a sufficiently large bowl with a small amount of hot water under the cage so that the steam can rise around the cage along the two long walls. (Do not remove the bottom pan of the cage!) Cover cage and water bowl with a light cloth so that the steam penetrates into the cage, but keep the infrared light directed at the bird. If your parakeet is housed in a very large cage you may have to move the bird to a small "hospital cage" for this treatment.

As a makeshift solution you can hang damp, hot towels around the cage except on the front and shine an infrared lamp into the front half of the cage. The towels should always be damp.

Caution: If you notice even the slightest convulsive movement or sign of paralysis, infrared radiation therapy is not advisable.

Treatment of Fractures

If your parakeet breaks a leg bone by getting its toes entangled, crashing to the ground, or enduring some other misfortune, you will notice the injured leg hanging down uselessly. A broken wing hangs uselessly and grounds the bird. In either case it would be best to take the bird to an animal clinic to check out the fracture with an X ray. If a leg fracture is below the feathered part of the leg—i.e., the leg, or tarsus, or the toes—there is no need for an X ray. Compound fractures, where the broken bone penetrates through muscle and skin and causes a bleeding wound, have to be treated by an avian veterinarian. Simple fractures of the toes need no special treatment; they heal by themselves. A leg fracture that has not broken the skin can be treated with a splint: Wrap a layer of gauze around the leg; cut a straw to the exact length needed for the splint; slit the straw lengthwise and fit it snugly around the leg; attach the straw with tape. Make sure the tape does not touch the skin, to avoid harm to the newly healed leg when you peel off the tape. The splint is left on for ten days for a simple fracture; after the splint is removed the bird will favor the weak leg until it is fully healed.

Theoretically, a fracture higher up on the leg or on the thigh should be treated with surgery. But since both the veterinarian and the bird's owner usually prefer to avoid such a serious operation, the entire leg is simply immobilized. The broken

Important Signs of Illness

Signs of illness	Possible cause	Treatment Page
Loss of a few feathers but without bald spots; increased pecking at feathers.	Molt; not a disease but necessary renewal of plumage.	57
Blood on feathers.	Injuries.	59
Getting caught in fabrics and on cage grating.	Claws too long.	59
Deformed bill.	Overgrowth of bill.	60
Dragging leg.	Leg fracture.	62
Drooping wing; inability to fly.	Broken wing.	62
Prolonged loss of feathers; bald spots; rough-looking plumage.	Ectoparasites such as red mites, feather mites, lice; nutritional deficiencies (vitamins and minerals); metabolic or hormonal disturbances.	65
Misshapen or discolored feathers; dull and often ragged plumage.	Not enough exercise; nutritional deficiency; hormonal disturbance; poor circulation; feather cysts.	66
Plucking of feathers; bald spots in the plumage.	Nutritional deficiency; allergy; boredom; loneliness.	66
Whitish gray, crusty layer on upper bill, on ceres, around eyes, on legs, and around vent.	Parrot mange.	68
Squeaking or rattling noises when breathing; difficulty getting air; whipping tail; regurgitating food; tossing of the head.	Infection of respiratory system with bacteria, viruses, or fungi; colds; crop inflammation; pneumonia; enlarged crop; change in thyroid gland; egg binding.	68
Dragging leg; toes in clenched fist position; paralysis of other body parts; cramps.	Lack of vitamins E and B; brain damage; concussion; tumors.	69
Diarrhea; droppings mushy, watery, slimy, fermenting, strongly discolored, or mixed with blood.	Colds; nutritional deficiency; poisoning; spoiled food; salty or spicy human food; nephritis; liver damage; tumors; infections.	70
Visible straining when passing stool; droppings hard, pale yellow, or gray, mixed with blood.	Constipation.	72
Straining in vain; shortness of breath, very large droppings (almost liquid, often with blood); exhaustion.	Egg binding.	72
Yellowish to brownish scabs on underside of wings, base of tail, and inside of thighs; general ailing state; increased thirst.	Eczema caused by fungi or other as yet unknown pathogens. Possibly a reaction to chemically treated feed or environmental factors.	75
Refusal to eat; diarrhea; shortness of breath; conjunctivitis with discharge of pus; crop inflammation; cramps; paralysis.	Psittacosis.	76

bones will then heal, though perhaps not perfectly lined up, and the bird will adjust to a minor deformity. Pull the toes and tarsus gently up to the body and tie them in place with a gauze bandage that runs underneath both wings. Tape the bandage tightly but as much as possible avoid attaching the tape to the feathers. When you remove the bandage after about two weeks, cut off the feather tips with tape on them first, then cut through the bandage and take it off. If quite a few feathers still stick to the tape, carefully remove them with a minimum of an acetone solvent or mineral spirits; make certain that there is adequate ventilation because the bird may pass out from the fumes.

Broken wings call for similar treatment. If there is no open wound, place the injured wing in its natural position and tie it in place with strips of gauze and tape. Wait three weeks before removing the bandage.

A bird with a broken leg or wing should be kept quiet in a small cage. Leave only

This is how you should tie a wing with a broken bone. The bird will need peace and quiet and should preferably be housed in a cage by itself.

two perches in the cage at a high enough level that the splinted leg can hang down unhindered. If a leg or wing is tied to the body the bird has to be able to get at its food with a minimum of exertion. As an aid to the healthy leg (or both legs in case of a broken wing) the bottom of the cage should be covered with clean, soft, and crumpled paper, and gravel supplied in a little dish. Calcium and vitamin supplements speed up the healing process.

The Band on the Bird's Leg

The band your parakeet may wear when you purchase it at the pet store (see page 15) is proof that the bird comes from a breeder who is a member of a parakeet society. However, this band is the source of many injuries and of constant minor discomfort to the bird. The band can easily catch in cloth or on other objects and thus cause a fracture or other injury. Because many parakeets never get used to this foreign object and keep fussing over it, the banded leg is subject to swellings, inflammations, rashes, and infestations of parasites. Once a problem has developed it is often difficult to remove the band. Should you decide that you don't want the band, entrust its removal only to an avian veterinarian.

Diseases That Can Affect Parakeets

Properly kept parakeets rarely get seriously sick. Miserable though your parakeet may look when suffering from one of the conditions described in the preceding table, and frightening as an external injury may appear to you, the little patient usually recovers quickly if you take prompt appropriate measures and get expert advice or assistance (avian veterinarian, experienced aviculturist, pet dealer). In these cases of quick recovery the underlying cause is often apparent. The situation, however, becomes truly harassing for both parakeet and owner if all the recommended home remedies bring only temporary relief or none at all and the veterinarian prescribes a broad-spectrum antibiotic for lack of an exact diagnosis.

The bird's keeper can tell that the parakeet is sick from the changes in behavior described on page 54 (see also the chart of Important Signs of Illness). But many of these symptoms, such as diarrhea, great weakness, difficulty in passing stool, slimy discharges, changes in the skin, discoloration of the ceres, paralysis, listlessness, lack of appetite, and misformed feathers, can point to different causes that are difficult to trace in so small an animal, and a specific diagnosis thus is impossible. None of this reduces the bird keeper's obligation to do everything possible to help the pet overcome whatever the disease might be.

Loss of Feathers

A change in a parakeet's plumage is usually fairly obvious, particularly if you have had a chance to observe your bird undergo a natural molt several times. You are dealing with an abnormal loss of feathers if your bird keeps shedding feathers, constantly and hastily preens itself, and pecks at feathers and skin. In time, bare spots appear in the sparse plumage, particularly on the head, abdomen, and the undersides of the wings.

Possible causes: Feather mites, lice, red bird mites, nutritional deficiencies, metabolic disorders, hormonal imbalances.

Feather mites—parasites about one millimeter long, of flattened shape, and often taking on the color of their host's plumage—and lice can be seen especially under the wings when one strokes gently against the feathers. Red bird mites attack the birds only at night and suck their blood. Restlessness at night is a sign of infestation. Brooding females and nestlings are in constant danger because it is always dark inside the nesting box. Red bird mites can cause adult birds to become anemic and quite often can fatally weaken nestlings. If you suspect red mites, drape a white cloth over the cage and nesting box at night. In the morning you can clearly see the red, dark red, or blackish-brown parasites on the underside of the cloth. During the day they hide in dark corners, cracks in wood, and other crannies.

Measures to take: Whether dealing with lice, depluming scabies mites, feather mites, or red bird mites, get an effective but not harmful disinfectant from your avian veterinarian or pet dealer. Take your parakeet or parakeets out of the cage or aviary and out of the nesting box as well and disinfect *all* objects the birds touch, the cage or aviary, and the entire surroundings. Discard all nesting materials and replace with new ones.

Important: Never apply the spray to the bird, even if it is supposedly harmless. Spray particles can get into the bird's nose, mouth, and eyes and be a serious threat. Treat birds only with a disinfecting powder recommended by an avian veterinarian or pet dealer and cover its nose and eyes carefully. Since disinfectants are often ineffective against the parasites' eggs, a second treatment is necessary after five days, and a third treatment, one week after that. This is not a pleasant task, but it is absolutely necessary.

Abnormal loss of feathers is harder to combat if it is not caused by pests. In this case you will have to carefully review the bird's living conditions and especially its diet. The veterinarian can recommend medications to strengthen the bird, but should also examine the bird thoroughly to detect other causes.

Deformed Feathers

New feathers growing in can be so different in shape and color as to gradually alter the entire appearance of the parakeet. Usually these abnormal feathers are dull, less colorful, and often ragged. The long wing and tail feathers as well as the smaller contour feathers remain stuck in their sheaths, with only a small brushlike tuft fanning out at the top. Or the feather tapers about halfway up and turns around its own axis in a corkscrew pattern. Or the feather fails to develop a tip, the branches on either side of the shaft forming two points on the outer edges of the vane. Or the feather gets frayed toward the top and loses its original color or turns dark.

Possible causes: A cage that is too small, too many toys and perches inside it, inadequate exercise, nutritional deficiencies, hormonal imbalances, inadequate circulation after injuries (fractures, sprains), feather cysts, or, in young birds, perhaps French molt.

Measures to take: The bird needs more freedom of movement, its diet has to be scrutinized, and the veterinarian should prescribe an appropriate tonic to strengthen the bird after having examined the bird for other possible causes. (Pet stores also have good tonics for birds.) Older female para-

keets are particularly subject to cysts in the feather follicles; soft lumps form under the skin. When the veterinarian lances the cysts, a cloudy liquid drains out, and feathers, often misshapen, that could not break through the skin are revealed.

Feather Plucking

This "bad habit" is well known in larger parrots and occurs more rarely in parakeets. The long-term consequences can be serious illness or even death. The birds keep plucking at their feathers and pull out a great many of them. Even though this hurts, in severe cases the pain is not enough to stop birds from plucking themselves completely bare.

Possible causes: There are different opinions about the nature of this disorder. Some think its causes are psychological (boredom, loneliness, fright); others ascribe it to nutritional deficiencies; and still others regard it as an allergic reaction. Sometimes an overweight bird begins to pluck feathers because its skin feels stretched uncomfortably tight— or the humidity may be too low, or the skin is itchy with dandruff.

Measures to take: Check the bird for parasites and skin disorders and provide treatment if indicated. Review diet and provide supplements; eliminate negative environmental factors, such as noise and distracting optical stimuli; and remedy neglect. Supply fresh branches for gnawing on; try introducing a second parakeet as a companion. Recent publications report success in reducing feather plucking through adding table salt or iron to the drinking water. The recommended dosage for a parakeet is ½ teaspoon of salt to 2 cups (½ liter) of water. An iron

Health Care and Parakeet Diseases

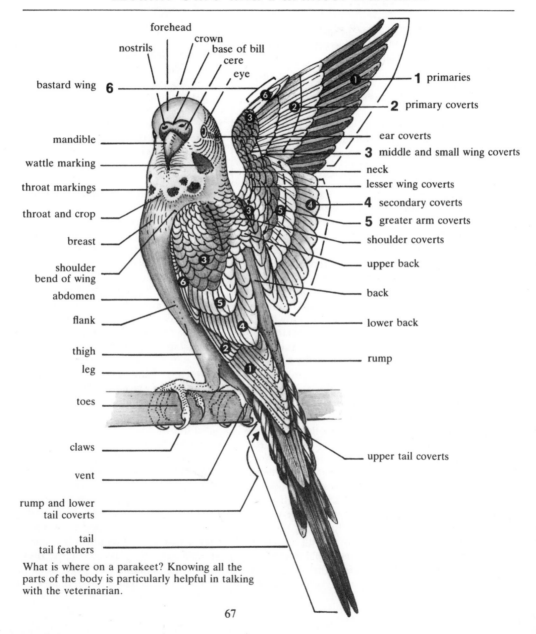

forehead
nostrils
crown
base of bill
cere
eye

bastard wing **6**

mandible
wattle marking
throat markings
throat and crop
breast
shoulder
bend of wing
abdomen
flank
thigh
leg
toes

claws
vent
rump and lower
tail coverts
tail
tail feathers

1 primaries
2 primary coverts
ear coverts
3 middle and small wing coverts
neck
lesser wing coverts
4 secondary coverts
5 greater arm coverts
shoulder coverts
upper back
back
lower back
rump

upper tail coverts

What is where on a parakeet? Knowing all the parts of the body is particularly helpful in talking with the veterinarian.

67

supplement or, as a last resort, an "Elizabethan" collar may be discussed with an avian veterinarian.

Scaly-face or Mycosis of the Beak

This first shows up as a spotty, grayish-white film on the upper mandible, starting at the corners of the beak and spreading sometimes to the ceres, the rims of the eyes, the legs, and the vent.

Possible cause: This disorder is caused by the tiny burrowing mite *Cnemidocoptes pilae*, which is present in passive form from nestling days and months or even years later can seriously affect a bird weakened by stress or other negative influences.

The mite burrows into the horny tissue of the beak or into the epidermis and feeds on skin particles and lymph. Sievelike tunnels destroy the skin, and the horny growths that appear are the bird's defense mechanism. The grayish film that shows up first can harden like scales and form welts and protrusions. In the initial stages this disorder bothers a parakeet very little, and it rarely spreads to other birds. Often the hardened growths fall off by themselves and they are not necessarily followed by other symptoms.

Measures to take: Since mycosis of the beak usually affects parakeets with temporarily weakened resistance, the bird's general state of health should be watched. Give the highest quality food and add a multivitamin solution to the drinking water. The visible film and growths should be gently dabbed with an antidote, but never with an oily contact insecticide, which could enter the circulatory system through the skin and be fatal. Many veterinarians recommend special

ointments or injections. In minor cases, balsam of Peru or Vaseline may be effective. Dab the affected spots with a Q-tip three times a day for three days, then twice a day every other day. Make very sure that none of the medication gets near the eyes, nose, or mouth. If the feet are affected, promptly remove the band, because the legs tend to swell, causing the band to cut off circulation. Loss of the foot is then possible.

Disorders of the Respiratory System

Parakeets are highly susceptible to these disorders. The first sign is that the bird becomes apathetic, loses interest in food, and possibly secretes a discharge from the nose. An attentive observer will notice that the parakeet has difficulty breathing and sometimes lifts the folded wings in an attempt to get air. In bad cases the bird gasps or pumps for air and sometimes will hang from a bar of the cage by the bill hoping to breathe easier through the stretched trachea. Sometimes squeaking or rattling noises are produced, and each breath may be accompanied by a simultaneous whipping of the tail. Occasionally the bird may try to get relief by choking up food and throwing it off with a toss of the head.

Possible causes: Unfortunately all these symptoms can occur with several different diseases. The respiratory system may be infected with bacteria, viruses, or fungi, and breathing difficulties, including strange noises, can also be caused by damaged air sacs, colds, crop inflammations, pneumonia, an enlarged crop, changes in the thyroid glands, egg binding (see page 72), and obesity. An exact diagnosis is extremely difficult

Health Care and Parakeet Diseases

A sick parakeet squats on a perch apathetically and puffed up; the tail droops down, and the belly rests on the perch. Shining an infrared lamp on the bird is a recommended first treatment.

with parakeets and often impossible while the bird is alive. But one of the most common causes of breathing difficulties is a crop inflammation caused by the ingestion of things that don't agree with the parakeet. The bird tosses its head back and forth in an effort to get rid of a brownish red discharge that then sticks to the feathers on the head. Inflammation of the crop is often accompanied by diarrhea; the bird feels very sick, looks miserable, and needs immediate attention from a veterinarian.

The much feared change in the thyroid glands leading to their enlargement actually occurs quite seldom. The efficacy of the much advertised, special iodine-enriched birdseed is questionable, because the birds seldom eat the "iodine kernels," and the entire question of the role of iodine in the body has not been sufficiently researched.

Measures to take: The first thing to do is to give the bird lukewarm, weak tea—black or chamomile—instead of water, and soft food made up of low-fat cottage cheese, hardboiled egg, and zwieback softened in water. The bird also needs uniform warmth and quiet. Extremely weakened birds should get, over a 24-hour period, nothing but glucose mixed with a vitamin preparation and a liver tonic recommended by the veterinarian or a pet dealer. Repeated injections by the veterinarian are often necessary to cure these extremely dangerous disorders.

Cramps and Paralysis

These symptoms develop so gradually that by the time measures are taken against them it is often too late. In any case, all that usually can be done is to try to correct possible vitamin deficiencies. This disorder affects primarily the legs and toes. At first all that you notice is a slight dragging of one leg, which the bird also favors visibly by pulling it up into the belly feathers. Gradually the nerves cease to function and the bird has difficulties holding on to a branch. The toes contract like a small fist. You can, however, open the fist gently with your fingers and place the toes around the perch. But as soon as the bird moves, the toes contract again into fist position.

Paralysis of other parts of the body is less common. If the movement of the wings is curtailed, this is usually the result of fractures or dislocation of a joint. But sudden paralysis of the entire body, often leading to loss of consciousness, does occur. Cramps, too, affect the legs first and can, in the absence of effective treatment, extend to the entire body and end in a painful death.

Possible causes: Cramps and paralysis can result from a deficiency of vitamins E and B, both highly sensitive substances that often survive in only minimal amounts in grains and seeds after long transport and subsequent storage.

Brain damage can lead to cramps and paralysis, but this is very rare.

Total paralysis, sometimes along with loss of consciousness, can be caused by a concussion that may be the result of a fall or collision (e.g., against a window).

In the majority of instances progressive paralysis is caused by growths or tumors. For reasons that are not yet sufficiently understood, parakeets seem to be getting progressively more susceptible to tumors. Since most of these tumors form inside the body cavity, they are hard to detect. The only indications of the problem are typical associated symptoms, such as paralysis (more rarely cramps) caused by pressure on nerves and blood vessels, often accompanied by diarrhea, discoloration of the ceres, and a general decline in the bird's health. Very large tumors can sometimes become apparent in the body contour by pressing against other organs.

Measures to take: If there is the slightest indication of paralysis or cramps, an avian veterinarian should be consulted immediately. Vitamin supplements always aid the overall health of a bird.

If a concussion has led to total paralysis, the bird should be kept in the dark and laid on something soft, with the head resting slightly higher than the body. When the bird regains consciousness, it should be kept at a uniform warm temperature, but not exposed to an infrared lamp. If recovery is not complete, consult the veterinarian.

If the paralysis is caused by a growth inside the body, chances of a cure are minimal, because the diagnosis is often too late and surgery rarely offers any hope. In the case of very weak, suffering birds, euthanasia is the most humane solution (see page 79).

Diarrhea

As already mentioned on page 54, short-term diarrhea is not necessarily a symptom of disease and may signal nothing more than passing physical or psychological discomfort. A healthy parakeet normally passes stool every ten to fifteen minutes, and the droppings consist of dark green to blackish rings that enclose white, creamy urine secretions. If a bird is excited, frightened, or otherwise upset, it tends to produce small droppings more often. Normal droppings dry and harden within a few minutes and can then easily be removed from a smooth surface. If the parakeet is perching on a branch, your shoulder, or inside its cage, it produces droppings without paying any attention, but if it happens to be tripping around on a surface it stays motionless for a few seconds to prevent the still loose stool from sticking to the feathers.

A marked change of consistency in the droppings over several days is a sign for alarm. The stool may be runny, watery, slimy, fermenting and strongly discolored, or even mixed with blood. If the bird also

Health Care and Parakeet Diseases

looks sick or weak, the stool should be analyzed as soon as possible. A veterinarian who is not set up to do this can tell you where to take or send the sample. The stool sample should be fresh and free of gravel. Either catch a dropping by holding a small plastic container under the bird or line the cage floor with clear plastic.

Important: The droppings of a female parakeet are often changed in appearance and softer before and during egg laying, and while the female sits on the eggs she produces noticeably less frequent, larger droppings. This is the result of hormonal changes and relieves the bird of having to interrupt incubation more often.

Possible causes: Almost all parakeet illnesses are accompanied by diarrhea. If stool analysis reveals no bacteria, parasites, or fungi, ask yourself the following questions:

• Could a cooler than usual bath, a draft, or a sudden drop in temperature have caused a cold?

• Is the bird getting too little grit, which is needed both as an aid to digestion and for the calcium it contains?

• Has the bird come in contact with anything harmful? One possibility is lead poisoning if the stool is slimy and a light red; another is poisoning caused by mildewy seeds, rotting fruit or vegetables, alcoholic or very salty and highly seasoned substances, toxic fumes, or poisonous house plants.

If these causes, too, can be eliminated, other illnesses that do not show up in the analysis of stool must be considered, such as chronic nephritis, liver disease, tumors, or infectious diseases.

Measures to take: If the cause is a cold, supply uniform warmth with an infrared lamp, sprinkle bird charcoal over the birdseed, and give the bird chamomile tea to drink. If there is no quick improvement, substitute 1 g of magnesium sulfate diluted in 30 ml of water for the chamomile tea.

In case of diarrhea, eliminate fruit and greens from the diet and make sure the bird gets plenty of liquid fortified with vitamins. If diarrhea lasts more than 24 hours, call an avian veterinarian.

Birds living in cages that do not have gravel at the bottom but are lined instead with "bird carpet," a kind of rough sandpaper that is supposed to wear the claws down, often do not get enough grit.

If there is any suspicion of poisoning it is best to consult the veterinarian immediately. As a first-aid measure you can give the bird a mixture of glucose, vitamin supplement, and a liver tonic. For lead poisoning there are injections that can save a bird's life. There is also a liquid antidote that may be prescribed if the bird is still willing to drink.

If a specific bacteriological infection has been diagnosed by the veterinarian, an antibiotic should be given strictly according to directions. Give the exact daily dosage determined for your bird and continue as long as indicated. If treatment is discontinued earlier because the bird seems to have recovered, the illness may return in a more virulent form and possibly no longer respond to the antibiotic.

If sulfa drugs are used to combat parasitic pathogens it is as important to follow directions for dosage and length of treatment as in the case of antibiotics. Also ask the veterinarian about vitamin supplements and liver tonic to improve the bird's general resistance.

Health Care and Parakeet Diseases

Constipation

This disorder is rare in parakeets. When a bird does have difficulty passing stool the keeper usually does not notice it right away. It is only when the bird obviously strains and moves it tail end back and forth in the effort, sometimes even emitting pitiful cries, that attention is called to its condition. If the bird does succeed, often with painful effort, to produce droppings, these may be of normal consistency but of larger quantity. Or the droppings may be hard, pale yellow or gray, and sometimes mixed with blood. Important: Female parakeets sometimes go through similar motions when laying eggs and may need prompt help if they are suffering from egg binding.

Possible causes: Incorrect diet, lack of exercise, reduced muscle tone because of obesity, ingestion of indigestible objects or of too much grit or bird gravel, pressure of an internal tumor on the intestines, or a growth in the vent.

Measures to take: Change the birdseed mixture, give more fruit, greens, and sprouts, make sure the bird has enough opportunity to fly and climb. As an emergency measure, withhold food for twenty-four hours; instead give the bird one drop of castor oil or wheat germ oil two or three times at intervals of three to four hours, inserting an eye dropper into the bill from the side and dripping the oil on the tongue. Treat the vent area with skin ointment. Add some Epsom salts to the drinking water at a ratio of 1:200. If there is no improvement within twenty-four hours, take the bird to the veterinarian immediately, because there may be a serious internal illness for which there is little chance of cure. In a severe case of constipation, euthanasia may offer the most humane relief from suffering (see page 79).

Egg Binding

Egg binding is the name given to difficulty in laying eggs and especially to the inability of a bird to press the egg out of the oviduct and the vent. The possibility of egg binding has to be considered if a female acts apathetic, produces droppings that are exceptionally large and too runny—often mixed with blood—whips her tail, and strains painfully. The bird seems nervous, keeps moving from perch to perch, and seeks relief by stretching the body and holding it almost horizontally. The careful observer will notice a slight roundness of the underbelly. If the egg is not passed within an hour when a female is in this state, she will quickly lose strength, look very ill, and squat on the cage bottom, barely able to keep her balance, plumage raised, eyes closed, emitting faint cries of pain. Without immediate help she will die.

Possible causes: Females that are too young may develop egg binding when they lay their first eggs, but even adults at the prime breeding age of one to two years can suffer from binding if the oviduct is not elastic enough or if the egg is too large.

An egg with too rough or too soft a shell or with no shell at all can also cause egg binding. So can poor nutrition, especially

Parakeets in artificially-bred color varieties. ▷
Above-left: Pied (harlequin) parakeet. Above right: Cinnamon parakeet. Below left: Pale blue parakeet. Below right: Lutino.

Health Care and Parakeet Diseases

vitamin and calcium deficiencies, housing in rooms that are too dark, damp, or cool, or too many broods in succession without adequate rest periods in between.

Measures to take: If the condition has not deteriorated to its most painful stage you can try to provide relief with damp heat (see page 61 for infrared radiation and hot steam). Also drip a little warmed castor oil or salad oil on the vent with an eye dropper every ten minutes. That is about all you can do. If the egg is not produced within two hours take the bird to the veterinarian. A vet who has experience with birds may try to assist the female's efforts with massage. If that fails there is a way to enlarge the oviduct without recourse to surgery, or an operation may be necessary. These last two measures can save the parakeet only if the exhaustion that goes along with egg binding is not too great. Important: Female parakeets kept singly or living with human-imprinted partners—in other words, birds that do not actually mate—sometimes lay eggs. It is best to give such a bird a nesting box for her eggs and let her sit for a time. If the eggs, which are infertile, are removed, the female may continue laying and get exhausted from this. This, too, can cause egg binding or an overall deterioration of health and serious illness.

Many a parakeet female living singly or in a platonic relationship with her partner lays eggs every six to eight weeks even if she is allowed to sit on them. I had such a bird

◁ A small sampling from the large assortment of birds offered by breeders. Parakeets come in all kinds of overall colors as well as with different markings.

who in the course of her nine years of life laid about 300 eggs and finally died of exhaustion. Hormone treatments administered at the bird clinic of a university were unsuccessful. Nowadays a veterinarian specializing in cage birds can cut the oviduct in a minor operation and thus prevent the useless exhausting production of eggs.

Eczema

In the past parakeets came down only occasionally with eczema that was usually caused by poor living conditions and inadequate diet. In recent years, however, the condition has occurred with increasing frequency even in birds that are excellently kept and fed. Patches of skin under the wings, near the base of the tail, and on the inside of the thighs are suddenly covered with a yellowish to brownish, crustlike substance that the birds peck off, causing the skin to redden and sometimes bleed. Often the birds give the impression of being sick but are restless at the same time and thirstier than usual.

Possible causes: Fungus infections can cause eczema of this type, but in recent times skin disorders have been appearing for which no pathogens are known. Veterinarians specializing in cage birds suspect that this may be an allergic reaction to birdseed that has been treated with chemicals or to some kind of environmental influences.

Measures to take: The only thing the bird's keeper can do is to provide the best possible living conditions and a varied diet rich in vitamins. Switch the birdseed mixture and add a multivitamin to the drinking water. A visit to the veterinarian is essential because the bird's entire organism has to be strengthened and its immune system activated. The veterinarian will prescribe a tincture, powder, or fat-free salve against the eczema. Ask if instead of an antibiotic a medication based on homeopathy could be prescribed, since homeopathy has scored some partial successes. Any success in treatment is likely to be only partial with the eczema found now. According to experience this skin disorder tends to recur, often in more virulent form, after a temporary improvement of the condition, and in many cases the bird's suffering can be relieved only through euthanasia.

Psittacosis

This infectious disease (also known as parrot fever and ornithosis) is named after parrots (Psittacidae) because it was first recognized when it broke out in humans who had been infected by sick, freshly imported parrots. Today we know that the disease also affects native songbirds, pigeons, and poultry and that these birds can be latent carriers. We speak of psittacosis in the case of parrots, ornithosis in the case of other birds, and parrot fever when humans have the disease. Strict health regulations have lessened the risk of human infections. The requirement to report all infected parrotlike birds, which applies even to all breeding operations including the hobby breeder, has reduced the dread this disease evoked at an earlier period. Fortunately effective methods of treatment and medications for this disease have been found. Human deaths caused by parrot fever are now very rare, and birds suffering from the disease no longer have to be killed but can be treated and often cured.

The pathogen responsible for psittacosis is named Chlamydia and is something between a virus and a bacterium. It can attack a parakeet either at the nestling stage or as an adult bird inhaling dust from the dried droppings of infected birds. The illness often remains latent but the pathogen is passed on in the droppings to other birds and to mammals, including humans. Unfortunately there

Eye inflammations are caused by drafts, dust, soot, and cooking vapors. The condition requires treatment by a veterinarian because there may be an infection.

are no unambiguous symptoms that clearly set psittacosis apart from other infectious diseases. Almost any parakeet with psittacosis stops eating. Often this is accompanied by diarrhea, inflammation of the crop, severe shortness of breath, catarrh of the nose and the intestines, purulent conjunctivitis, and, in severe cases, cramps and paralysis. If people come down with parrot fever they develop flulike symptoms that ultimately develop into something like pneumonia. The disease is not without danger for humans, and medical treatment is called for at the first sign.

Possible causes: Unclean conditions, poor diet, too little fresh air and exercise, a change in environment, transport, impaired condition because of a basically harmless illness or because of molt, unhappiness as a result of loneliness, the death of a partner, or neglect on the part of the keeper can all contribute to an acute outbreak of the latent disease. It happens quite often that a parakeet that has been kept as an only bird for years suddenly comes down with acute psittacosis because of a latent Chlamydia infection going back to nestling days. The contagion can also spread from wild birds to the birds in an outdoor aviary. In such a case humans too can be endangered.

Measures to take: Since at the acute stage of the disease the pathogen can be detected in the stool, a sample should immediately be analyzed if the described symptoms occur. Veterinary treatment is essential, and, for the owner's safety, the sick bird is moved to a special animal clinic to be treated there. The veterinarian or the health officials will let the owner know what further measures should be taken.

The Trip to the Veterinarian

A conscientious bird owner takes a sick parakeet to an avian veterinarian even if the medical treatment is likely to be more expensive than the cost of purchasing the pet.

Unfortunately there is no guarantee that the veterinarian's efforts will be successful. Very few veterinarians have studied the diseases of cage birds in detail, let alone those specifically affecting parakeets. All too often

the treatment is experimental. That is why I urge all keepers of parakeets to find a specialist in bird diseases before the need strikes. Ask at the pet store when you buy bird food or accessories, and strike up conversations with other customers there. If there is a veterinarian who knows about birds, word will spread quickly among bird fanciers.

To assist as much as possible in diagnosing a condition, take the bird to the veterinarian in its regular cage but protected against cold and dampness. The bird gravel should be replaced with clean paper so that the state of the droppings is clearly visible. You will also have to answer the following questions:

● How old is the bird?

● Where did you buy the bird? What breeding establishment does it come from? How long have you owned it, and who was the previous owner?

● When did you first notice that the bird looked sick?

● What symptoms (see page 42) have you observed and what changes from normal behavior?

● Has the bird been sick before? Was a specific illness diagnosed, and how was it treated?

● What birdseed mixture are you giving your bird? (Be sure to bring a sample.) What does the bird get to drink?

● What supplemental foods are you providing?

● What other animals live in your household?

● Is everybody in the family healthy?

Only with all this information can the veterinarian get an accurate first picture of the bird and possibly point out mistakes in care. An analysis of the stool for bacteria and parasites is also a must. If the veterinarian is not equipped to do this, get the name of a laboratory. You may want to take a fresh stool sample there yourself to get the results as quickly as possible.

If the stool sample does not reveal any sign of pathogens, ask the veterinarian to do whatever examinations might yield a diagnosis, such as X rays and biopsies of secretions, skin, or tissue. But make sure your parakeet is not treated like a laboratory animal. Make sure every suggested step is explained in detail and ask specifically if the step is absolutely necessary, what are the risks and hoped-for results, and what might happen if you refuse consent.

If the veterinarian suggests medication, stick minutely to the recommendations on how to give the medicine, on dosage and frequency, and on how long to continue giving it (see How to Give Medicines Properly, below). It would be irresponsible to experiment here. Ask the veterinarian to suggest all measures you can take involving diet, general care, heat or infrared therapy, to aid the treatment.

How to Give Medicines Properly

When you take your sick parakeet to the veterinarian, ask to have all proposed treatments and their possible effects fully explained to you. Medical treatment can work only if it is carefully followed. In giving medication it is important to follow instructions exactly. If the medication is added to the drinking water, the bird must not have access to any other source of water. Dripping faucets and bath water are off limits for

the time being, and fruit and greens are excluded from the diet now because they might quench the bird's thirst. If the medication is sprinkled or dribbled on the birdseed, the dish should be only partially filled, because a clever parakeet may knock the top layer of seeds out of the dish with its bill to avoid the perhaps distasteful or merely un-

Medications that cannot be added to the bird's food or water are dripped on the bird's tongue with a plastic syringe that is carefully introduced into the bill from the side.

familiar taste of medicine and to get at the seeds underneath. If the medication has to be given through the bill, first catch the bird as described on page 60, but hold it so it tilts slightly backward, and very carefully drip the required number of drops onto the tongue from the side. This is easier with thick liquids than with thin ones because the liquid must not get into the windpipe, where it could cause suffocation. If the bird resists and clamps its bill shut, try gently to slide your fingernail between upper and lower mandible and then slowly pry the bill open.

If the ailing parakeet shares a cage with a healthy one ask the veterinarian whether it is harmful for the healthy bird to eat and drink the medicated food and water. If the answer is yes, the healthy bird has to be moved to a separate cage so that the two can be fed separately. It is always the healthy bird that gets moved, because the sick bird should not be put under the strain of having to adjust to different surroundings.

Putting a Bird to Death

Only a veterinarian should put a pet to death, and only in cases where the continued existence of the animal would endanger others or would be nothing but torture for the creature involved. But since the law regards pets merely as property many veterinarians will kill a perfectly healthy bird for a fee if the owner claims to be allergic to the pet. The decision is therefore left up to the individual's conscience. Before you take this step, however, keep in mind that many animal shelters have large aviaries for escaped parakeets where these birds are kept in a flock and are often quite happy. If termination of your pet's life is necessary, having the veterinarian put the bird to sleep is the only defensible method.

Breeding Parakeets

The Beginnings of Parakeet Breeding in Europe

The first parakeet that Europeans had a chance to set eyes on was only a stuffed one, but it was nevertheless a sensational event for ornithologists when this bird was displayed in 1831 at the museum of the Linné Society in London. It took nine more years before the English scientist John Gould managed to bring the first live parakeets from Australia to England. Gould's brother-in-law succeeded in breeding some of these birds, and a London bird dealer sold the first pair of parakeets for the amazing sum of 27 pounds sterling, which would translate into a modern value of at least several hundred dollars.

The Antwerp zoo in Belgium was the first place where these small parakeets could be seen in captivity. In Antwerp, at the time the center of trade in cage birds, bird auctions as far away as Berlin and St. Petersburg were organized. In Antwerp the breeding of parakeets on a larger scale began around 1850, and soon a "parakeet craze" swept over Europe; France alone imported 100,000 pairs a year. Since the breeding establishments in Holland and Belgium could not meet the huge demand for this cute small parrot, masses of wild parakeets were imported into Europe. Crowded into small cages, deprived of their accustomed food, many birds perished on the long journey by sea. But the popularity of the parakeet grew so rapidly that new shipments were sent off more and more frequently. The Australian government grew alarmed over the decimation of the native bird populations and in 1894 placed a parakeet export embargo (still in force today). This move did not, however, hinder the growing popularity of these birds, for by 1894 there were successful hatcheries in France and Belgium. In southern France, for instance, two hatcheries were set up in 1880 and 1886, with between 80,000 and 100,000 birds. In Germany, Countess von Schwerin first succeeded in breeding parakeets as early as 1855.

It is not surprising that among the innumerable parakeets that were bred in Europe there were some birds whose plumage color differed from that of the wild birds. In 1872 the first yellow parakeets appeared in Belgium, and in 1875 Germany had some too. Lutinos were first bred in Belgium in 1879. The first pure blue parakeets go back to 1878, white ones to 1917, and the Danish harlequins or Danish pied to 1940. All these different strains are mutations of the wild parakeet, i.e., a change has taken place in the genes that determine the coloration of the plumage (see page 102). The palette of colors has grown so large because breeders never tire of inventing new shades. I can only hope that their ambitions are always coupled with a concern for the health and innate needs of these pretty, small parrots (see page 53).

Requirements for Breeding

Many keepers of parakeets who have watched their birds bill and coo together and preen each other or have seen the male busily feed his mate would like to raise some baby birds. But they don't quite know what to do to encourage their birds to breed. Breeding parakeets—or rather, increasing their number (see Playing with Colors, page

Breeding Parakeets

A parakeet embodying current breeding standards. The domestic "ideal" is clearly bigger and heavier than the "wild" one (right).

A parakeet in the wild. This bird and the domesticated bird (left) are of a similar species.

98)—is quite easy if some basic requirements are met. Among these, optimal care and conditions—as described earlier in this book—are just as important as the specialized knowledge I would like to convey in this and the following sections.

Most aviculturists recommend banding parakeets when they are seven to nine days old. I myself don't band my birds until they start leaving the nesting box (see page 93) to make sure they don't hurt their legs with the band (see illustration on page 93 for banding birds).

One more important consideration: Ask yourself *before* you set out to raise parakeets what is to happen to the young birds when they grow up. Remember that if even two pairs mate simultaneously, a short time later a dozen or so birds will chirp and twitter in your home or outdoor aviary. Noise-sensitive neighbors may be far from enthusiastic about this. In the worst case you may be taken to court and forced to get rid of the birds. If you have ambitious breeding plans it would therefore be best to consult your neighbors before you get started.

Breeding Parakeets

Choosing Your Breeding Stock

If you don't yet own a pair of parakeets that you want to breed, buy two young birds of the same age from different pet dealers. This way you can be fairly sure that the birds come from different hatcheries, are therefore genetically different, and inbreeding is unlikely. (Inbreeding has to be avoided at all cost if you raise birds commercially.) Just to be on the safe side, ask for the name of the breeder who supplies each pet store, because sometimes one breeder sells to several stores.

Although parakeets are sexually mature after a few months (see page 111), you should not let them breed until they reach the age of ten or twelve months. The advantage of this is that the birds have reached their full size and are strong enough to withstand the physical strain of raising young, which also benefits the brood. (Foiling parakeets eager to mate is not easy, however. See page 98.)

Do not breed any birds with obvious defects, such as deformed feet, a misshapen bill, or imperfect plumage. If you buy a mate for a parakeet you already own you should still choose a young bird, because an older one might no longer be suitable for mating because of previous experiences that affect normal behavior (for example, human-imprinted birds, see page 85). Anyone wanting to breed for certain traits, such as color, has to take genetic background into consideration when choosing birds (see page 101).

In my opinion banded birds can be placed right after purchase in an aviary with other birds already in it. But cautious breeders first house newly acquired birds in a sepa-rate cage (within sight and hearing of their fellows). This gives the keeper a better chance to observe if the new bird is really healthy, and it allows the parakeet to get adjusted in peace to its new surroundings.

As a biologist and long-term friend of parakeets I strongly disfavor the present trend of breeding exceptionally large and heavy parakeets, because this represents a drastic departure from the size and build of wild parakeets. The flying ability of these cage birds is significantly reduced, and they tend more to obesity, which also means that they are more susceptible to disease.

The breeding for very specific traits in animals is often harmful to the organism. The goals of parakeet breeding are not determined by economic factors as is the case in animal husbandry (and even there controversy is arising) but by aesthetic considerations. It is therefore in order to question whether it makes sense or is even justifiable to deliberately alter by genetic manipulation a creature that is naturally so beautiful and that has achieved optimal adaptation to the environment of its homeland (see page 111). It seems to me that birds bred in captivity should have all the qualities theoretically needed to survive were they to be released in their native biotope. In any case, I urge any budding parakeet breeder with the goal of achieving specific traits (whether in the coloration or the shape of the birds) not to engage in amateur experimentation but to study genetics (see page 101). Also make use of the experiences (both good and bad) of conscientious experts (see Useful Addresses, page 136).

Brerding Parakeets

The Nest Box

If after thinking it over carefully you decide you *do* want to raise parakeets and have obtained the necessary permit, the next step is to buy a nest box to place in the spacious cage. The minimum space *one* pair of parakeets needs to raise young is a cage 24 inches long, 12 inches wide, and 16 inches tall (62 × 30 × 40 cm. See illustration on page 16). Two or more pairs need a correspondingly larger cage or an aviary (see page 23). Parakeets brood in cavities; in their native Australia they use cavities in trees. Since they do not build nests but make do with bare cavities (see page 113), you do not have to supply nesting materials.

Pet stores sell nest boxes that suit parakeets. The box should be 5½ inches high, 7 inches deep, and 10 inches long (14 × 18 × 25 cm; see illustration below). These measurements are, of course, nothing more than guidelines. If you can find only bigger or smaller boxes, choose a larger one where the nestlings will have more room to

Nest box for parakeets. The top can be lifted so that you can check on activities inside the box.

move around. Also the air circulation is better, which is important for the clutch.

The shallow nest hollow should not be directly beneath the entry hole but a little to the side (see illustration on left). That way the female will not land on the eggs or nestlings when she hops into the box. Other important features are a landing perch (females prefer boxes with such a perch) and a top that flips up (to make cleaning easier, see page 83). It is easy to build such a box yourself and very practical if you construct it so that both top and back wall can be removed (a feature not found in commercially available boxes).

One researcher has shown convincingly in a scientific study that the size of the entry hole plays a role in whether parakeets accept certain nest boxes. Parakeet pairs were given a choice between boxes with entry holes measuring 1, 1½, and 2 inches (2.5, 3.5, and 5.5 cm), respectively. The females all chose the 1½-inch hole, and observation of parakeets in the wild shows that, they too, if there is a chance, select tree hollows with entries about that size.

In my opinion it is better to mount the box outside the cage. Then the birds have full use of the space they are accustomed to, and they are not bothered by the keeper's checking on the eggs. If you want to attach a nesting box on the outside of a cage that does not have a door in the side wall, hang the box directly on the bars with two hooks and nip off a few of the bars with wire cutters so that the birds can slip in unhindered. When the brood has left the nest, simply close off the hole in the wall with some wire mesh. (Cages with side doors, shown in illustration on page 16, are available commercially.)

Breeding Parakeets

The cage should be approximately at human eye level so that the contact between keeper and birds is maintained during the brooding period. The cage should not be near a radiator, because it is too dry and warm there and the fertile eggs can dry out. I would recommend letting the birds brood in a well-aired (draft-free!), not too shady room at normal indoor temperatures. This is the most favorable environment for hatching parakeets, even though these birds are remarkably hardy and immune to cold weather (see page 108). In the institute where I used to work, the parakeets had access from their heated shelter to an outdoor aviary. It was exhilarating to watch them bill and coo and go through their courtship displays outdoors even in the deep of winter. The birds were obviously enjoying themselves. This is not to say, of course, that you can impose just about anything on your parakeets, as I have, unfortunately, seen done by some large-scale breeders who let their birds hatch in dark and dank cellars or in outdoor aviaries without any shelter at all. As in any other profession there are among bird breeders a few unscrupulous individuals who seem to have no sensitivity for the creatures in their charge.

If you have several pairs that are going to breed in an aviary you obviously hang the nesting boxes inside the aviary. To avoid conflicts between the females, make sure the boxes are not too close to each other. I find a distance of about five feet between boxes is ideal. If the distance is less than that a strange female may keep perching in front of a box that is already occupied and interfere with the brooding.

The Australian biologist Edmund Wyndham observed in wild parakeets that birds nesting in the same tree got along peacefully as long as the entries to the different tree holes were at least three feet apart.

It is also good to have several boxes for every pair to choose from and to hang them as high as possible. (If the boxes are all alike, domesticated parakeets favor those that are higher up.)

One more reminder: It is essential that fresh drinking water always be available, because baby parakeets develop very quickly and have a high requirement for fluids not always met through food intake.

Matching a Pair

With many birds, large parrots, for example, matching a male and female is something of a gamble because of individual antipathies. Luckily this is not true of parakeets: Generally a pair will get along well after a certain period of adjustment. If it should happen that two birds fail to make friends, either because the female refuses to accept the male or because the male shows no interest in the intended mate, replace one of the partners with a new bird—assuming you have more than just one pair.

You can also introduce a second male that may get along better with the female. But not vice versa! Adding another female is usually disastrous, because females tend to fight each other. Conflicts between two males, on the other hand, are rare. The female simply chooses one of them as a mate, which the other accepts without grudge.

Difficulties can also arise if a bird was exposed exclusively to humans during a spe-

Breeding Parakeets

cific phase of development in which sexual imprinting takes place. Imprinting happens only during a very limited sensitive period in an animal's life, the timing of which differs for each species. We do not know yet exactly when sexual imprinting occurs in parakeets. The days immediately after the eyes open, i.e., about after the tenth day, seem to be of importance in imprinting. This is what Professor Roger Stamm and the biologist U. Blum concluded in a study they published. They observed that a blue male that had lived with green parents until it was seventeen days old and then moved in with blue stepparents and blue siblings later chose green birds as mates.

The famous writer on animal behavior, Konrad Lorenz, first wrote about this special form of learning, imprinting. In this process animals can "learn" the most absurd things: Male turkeys have been sexually imprinted to cardboard boxes and females to humans, and later the animals would address their courtship displays to these inappropriate "partners" and try to mate with them.

I have heard many tales of male parakeets that refused to take the slightest notice of a female partner and would even chase her around in the cage and hack at her. Whenever I inquired into the details it turned out that these birds had been exceptionally tame and friendly and that they would quite often regurgitate some undigested kernels from the crop into the keeper's hand. Spitting up kernels this way is a sign that the bird is courting the owner. This unnatural behavior thus indicates that the parakeet was probably wrongly imprinted and now regards humans as sexual partners.

If a male parakeet really is imprinted to humans, in most cases it makes little sense to try to use him for breeding. My pet bird Purzel, however, which I had during my student days and which was responsible for wakening my interest in parakeets, used to regurgitate seeds as described. I must admit that at the time I didn't think much about it until I heard in a lecture one day that parakeets are extremely gregarious birds. From that moment there was no doubt in my mind that Purzel should have a female friend. To my amazement Purzel paid no attention to his Jenny. Luckily he didn't attack her because if he had I would surely have separated the two. That would have been a mistake because about one year later he began to court her, and the two birds successfully raised several broods.

The Choice of a Mate

Like 90 percent of all birds, parakeets are monogamous. How permanent the bond to one mate is varies from species to species; it can last for one or several mating cycles or be for life. In the case of parakeets the bond lasts for life. If you have several pairs of birds in an aviary you can see this for yourself. Once two birds have mated they are usually "faithful" to each other. Fritz Trillmich, a biologist at the Max Planck Institute for the Study of Animal Behavior in Seewiesen, has studied this "marital fidelity" and was able to show that even after a seventy-day separation parakeets will resume their relationship with the old partner if they have been kept in the meantime with birds *of the same sex*. Even after a twenty-day separation during which a bird is kept together with other potential sexual part-

Breeding Parakeets

ners, the original bond is maintained. These observations are of practical interest to aviculturists: If, after raising a brood, two birds that have formed a bond have to be separated to keep them from going through the mating cycle too often (see page 98) the keeper can fairly assume that they will accept each other again unproblematically later. On the other hand, parakeets usually adjust with relative ease to a new partner if a bird has to be replaced or if the breeder wishes to mate a specific pair.

If you have several parakeets in an aviary it is of course important to know according to what criteria mates are chosen. "Love at first sight" apparently does not exist among parakeets; instead they choose a partner who seems to offer the best prospects for reproduction. This is the conclusion—rather prosaic from the human perspective—that the biologist Urs Engesser reached. His observations of parakeets showed that young females quite early favor older males for mates rather than males of their own age, even though the young females had close social bonds to the males they grew up with (see page 117). Young males, on the other hand, prefer females that have already claimed a nesting box, something females do even before being committed to a partner.

Females remain passive in the early stages of partner choice. The males court them, and if a female does not care for a particular admirer she hacks at him or threatens him. If she does like him, she rubs beaks with him or the two preen each other's feathers.

The two sexes are ready to mate at different ages: males about 130 days after leaving the nesting box, and females after 112 days.

Courtship and Mating

By their courtship behavior you can tell when two birds have accepted each other. Courtship behavior, or courtship display, is the collective term for all behavior leading up to the actual mating. Parakeets make charming pairs. They often sit together, preen each other, and rub beaks. It is the male who initiates the mating by going through his courtship display to arouse the female sexually: Both are sitting close to each other, and the male starts singing to his beloved while puffing up the feathers on his head and throat. As he sings he moves away from the female a couple of inches, then moves closer again and taps his bill against hers several times in succession. This performance is repeated several times with growing excitement, visible in the rapid bobbing of the head. The pupils of the eyes are narrowed, and the plumage on head and throat is still puffed up.

Feeding the female is part of the male's courtship display. The bills of the two birds are hooked together at right angles (see illustration on page 35) as the male chokes up food from his crop.

This display feeding—which is part of the mating ritual in many bird species—serves the purpose of pacifying the female and also allows the male to stay next to her and, if possible, to mount her. Females are often aggressive toward males before the courtship display or try to flee, and the ritual feeding calms their fear and aggressiveness.

If the male's wooing is successful, the female assumes the copulating position (see illustration on right). She looks almost transfixed, with the head thrown back, the head feathers slightly puffed, the wings held close,

Breeding Parakeets

A female ready to mate. If a male's courtship is successful, this is the posture she assumes.

and the tail feathers raised up in the air. (She does not change her position during mating.) This stance is a signal for the male to mount the female. But first he hesitates a moment. Then he approaches her from the side at a right angle, cautiously lifts one leg, and then briefly stands on her back on one foot. After this "foreplay" he climbs up with both legs, lowers his tail, and moves back and forth sideways. Since the tail feathers of the female are raised high, the cloacas of the two birds can touch. Now the male spreads one wing over the female (see color photo on page 127) and executes the copulating motions.

To my knowledge this spreading of the wing over the female is unique among birds. Presumably this posture helps both partners keep their balance during mating, for young and inexperienced parakeets often lose their balance. The difficulties usually arise in the first phase of copulation: either when the male mounts the female or when he tries to press his cloaca against hers. Before falling off, the male often tries to right himself by hooking his bill into the female's. Usually these difficulties are overcome after a few tries, generally after the first or second day. Difficulties sometimes persist, however, if the birds have been kept singly too long or are wrongly imprinted (see pages 84 and 122). Difficulties could also be due to perches that are too smooth.

Partnerless males still engage in display behavior, courting surrogates such as a shiny holder of a water dish or other objects sticking out from a wall. Courtship behavior is stimulated in parakeets primarily by factors such as diet and the presence of nesting boxes, as well as the company of other parakeets (see page 112), so that there is usually no problem inducing this behavior in birds kept under optimal conditions in an aviary.

Occasionally a single pair of parakeets refuse to show any interest in mating even though the setup seems perfect. This is because parakeets naturally live in flocks and the presence of other pairs stimulate sexual behavior. Laboratory examinations have shown that the testes and ovaries are larger in birds that could see and hear other pairs than in ones that had no contact with other birds. (Testes and ovaries produce the substances that trigger courtship behavior; see page 111).

To encourage a reluctant pair to mate, introduce a second pair of birds. But please make sure the cage is spacious enough (see page 83). If it is not, you may be able to borrow a pair of parakeets (in their own cage) from an acquaintance until your own birds are started on the mating cycle. Once your birds have raised a brood this difficulty is taken care of for good.

One more bit of advice: Borrow birds from a keeper who also wants a new brood of parakeets. As a result of mutual stimulation the borrowed birds, too, may start a new family.

Egg Laying and Brooding

In parakeets the choice of a nesting box is entirely up to the female. In cockatiels, it is up to the male. A female that has a mate and is ready to nest will approach a nesting box within minutes of having been mounted. The first visit to the box is very brief; the female will reemerge instantly and fly off. The next inspection is longer, and the inside walls and nest hollow (see illustration on page 83) where the eggs will later be deposited are examined by gnawing. Gradually the female spends more and more time inside the box, but she still responds suspiciously to any disturbance. At the slightest sound and sometimes without any apparent reason she will raise her head to the entry hole or stick her head out. If there is a major interference (too much activity in the room or loud noises), she immediately leaves the box. It is thus important to avoid anything that might disturb her, because otherwise the female will look for a new nesting box (in an aviary) or refuse to return to the box. Even if she does return she does not fully resume her broodiness (readiness to incubate eggs). The reason for this sensitivity to noise and other disturbances may be explained by the fact that, in parakeets as in other birds, broodiness and the maturing of the eggs in the ovaries are controlled by

hormones. These hormones become active only after the female has spent some time in the dark nesting cavity and has been exposed to her mate's song. It is therefore extremely important for the successful raising of offspring not only that the female be able to "take over" her nesting box in peace but also that she hear her partner well.

The female's behavior changes dramatically after she has laid her first eggs. The eggs appear one at a time at intervals of one or two days until there is a clutch of three to five eggs (sometimes more). An egg weighs about two grams, is white (as with most birds that brood in cavities), blunt-ended, and has a dull shell. If you have the opportunity to watch a female lay an egg you will realize what a strain this is for her. The egg is pushed out through the mighty pressure of the muscles associated with the oviduct. After expelling the egg the bird remains rigid and motionless for about five minutes, breathing rapidly, wings stretched out, and tail feathers bent downward.

If a female suffers from egg binding (see page 72), extreme caution is in order because this may be fatal. Watch the bird carefully during the entire egg-laying period, because you can treat egg binding successfully only if you act immediately.

Incubation starts after the first egg is laid, and usually the female does all the brooding. If there are unfamiliar noises she will still peer out of the entry hole but usually does not leave the box. The brooding instinct is so strong now that she continues sitting on the eggs even when the keeper lifts the top of the box to look in. This should be done very cautiously and without any abrupt movements. The female now leaves the box only to deposit droppings, which she does considerably less often than normal (normal means every twelve to fifteen minutes). But the stool pellets are considerably heavier than usual; they can weigh up to 10 percent of the bird's body weight.

The male feeds the female during the entire incubation period. To do so he sits on the perch in front of the entry hole, and the female sticks her head out of the hole to have him "stuff" her bill.

You can check to see if all the eggs are fertile, but preferably when the female is off the clutch (depositing droppings). An infer-

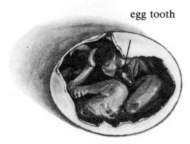

egg tooth

Position of the embryo inside the egg shortly before hatching.

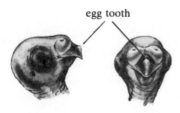

egg tooth

The chick pecks open the egg shell with its egg tooth, a calcareous, thornlike protrusion on the upper mandible.

tile egg looks translucent if held up against the light after about ten days. Fertile eggs show a bluish opaqueness and look a little darker. Remove infertile eggs only if the clutch is large (more than four eggs), because the female can probably tell with her brood patches—i.e., almost bare patches with good blood circulation on the breast—when the number of eggs is significantly reduced. Such a change could confuse her enough to make her give up brooding.

When the female returns to the nest she "checks" the eggs, feeling them over with her tongue and sometimes rolling them over with her bill. A female parakeet cannot tell her own eggs from those of other parakeets. If strange eggs are put in the nesting cavity they are rolled and brooded like her own. This means that eggs from different clutches can be interchanged without problems. Or you can exchange an infertile egg for a fertile one from an abandoned clutch.

Incubation (the time between the laying of the eggs and the hatching) generally lasts eighteen days. During this period the female keeps turning the eggs, changing their position in the nest so that they are all kept equally warm. This turning of the eggs is just as important for the development of the embryo as the correct temperature and humidity in the nesting box. The bird room (or aviary) should not be too cold, should get plenty of fresh air, and should have a humidity of about 60 percent.

I strongly urge you to leave the clutch alone and not try to clean eggs that have gotten dirty from the droppings of already hatched fellow nestlings. If an egg is handled improperly the embryo might come to harm; in addition the cleaning destroys the waxlike film that protects the egg against infections.

Breeding Parakeets

The Hatching of the Baby Birds

Hatching is a critical moment in the development of a baby bird. The hatchling has to work hard to make its way out of the shell, and the effort is not always successful. The mother bird meanwhile has to change over from sitting on eggs to taking care of nestlings. This transition is not as easy as you might think. But the mother bird gets some warning in the form of cheepings coming from the chicks inside the shells. About twenty-four hours before hatching, the parakeet chick starts making chirping and cracking sounds. This is a signal for the mother bird to check the eggs more frequently. She gets up and feels the surface of the eggs with her tongue, looking for the first holes in the shell. Like other baby birds, a parakeet chick pecks against the shell with its egg tooth (a calcareous, thornlike protrusion on top of the upper beak; see illustration on page 89). Then it turns a fraction of an inch and pecks again, creating a small crack in the thin shell. After a lot of painstaking and hard work—pecking, turning, pecking, craning of the neck—half the shell flips open like the hinged lid of a box. With further stretching, now of the wings and legs, the hatchling finally emerges completely. Meanwhile the parakeet mother does not remain idle; she keeps getting up, bends over the eggs, and, when she finds a crack, reaches in with her bill and sometimes moves the egg from under her. I have also observed different behavior: When a chick moved (the edges of the shell would open and then close again) some parakeet mothers would start nibbling along the crack and break off pieces of shell. Others would only feel the spot where the chick was visible and then settle down again

The mother bird picks up the egg by the hole the chick has pecked . . .

and proceeds to break off pieces of the shell . . .

until the chick is freed and is able to emerge from the shell.
(Drawn after a series of photographs taken by the author.)

90

Breeding Parakeets

on some or all of the eggs.

Most of the newly hatched, naked, and blind chicks find their own way back under the mother's feathers, and others are pushed back by her. The mother breaks down the shell "lid" by pecking at it, then turns to the rest of the empty shell and eats the egg skin. Finally she gets rid of the shell remnants by kicking them out of the nest hollow into a corner of the nesting box. Some time later the pieces of shell are thrown out of the box altogether (especially in tall and narrow boxes with less floor area than the wider ones I recommend). It is important for the shells to be cleared out of the nest hollow so that freshly hatched chicks don't get hurt on the sharp edges. One time I saw a chick accidentally crawl back head first into the empty egg instead of under the mother. It kicked frantically and cheeped but was unable to free itself without help. The mother didn't react at all, obviously not "knowing" what to do in such a situation since the hatching phase was already over. After a few minutes I stepped in to free the unhappy chick from its predicament.

The chicks hatch in the order in which the eggs were laid, one about every other day (see page 89). Thus in a clutch of five eggs the last chick is likely to appear when the first one is about ten days old. The process of hatching takes about twenty minutes, and a newborn chick weighs about 2 grams.

Some chicks are apparently unable to turn in the egg and therefore peck only a small hole in the shell (see illustration on left top). These chicks are not strong enough to break open the shell and would perish if the mother didn't come to their aid by breaking off more of the shell until the chick can finally get out. The drawings on page 90

illustrate three phases of this amazing process.

To find out more about the female's behavior I experimented and simulated the sounds and movements a chick makes inside an egg and the appearance of the egg during the hatching phase. (The mere mention of "experiment" these days often evokes outrage, but be assured that none of my charges came to harm.) With a razor blade I carefully cut a hole into the shell of an infertile parakeet egg and smuggled the egg in with the clutch of a brooding female. She paid no attention to the "doctored" egg and continued brooding. I now played a tape of a chick cheeping inside the egg in preparation for hatching. The mother bird reacted to the sound on the tape by looking the eggs over more often but did not start nibbling at the shell of my carefully prepared egg. The calls stimulated her only to keep checking but not to start nibbling on the shell. I had to find other factors that would evoke this latter behavior. When I once picked up an egg with a chick in the process of hatching (please don't try this yourself because you can easily cause harm by interfering at this point) I clearly felt the movements of the chick inside the egg. Now I knew I had to simulate this movement inside my doctored egg if I wanted to continue my experiment. I tried all kinds of devices based on physics—without success—and after six months of trial and error, when I was on the point of giving up, I happened to come across some Mexican jumping beans. They are seeds that have small larvae of a certain kind of moth inside them. Under the influence of warmth these larvae move so vigorously that the bean starts "jumping." I took one of these beans and slipped it into my special egg, and

91

Breeding Parakeets

now I was able to observe the female parakeet nibble on the doctored egg after sitting on it for a while (supplying the necessary warmth for the larvae) just as if the egg had a chick inside it. Here was proof that the cries of the chick inside the egg cause the mother bird to check the eggs more often but that it takes the "kicking" of the chick to make her break off pieces of the shell. Of course it also proved that the mother bird is not motivated by the conscious desire to help the chick at this precarious stage but acts out of pure instinct. This was shown, too, by another incident. A chick had already made a big crack in the egg but died—presumably from weakness—in the process of hatching. But the mother bird kept nibbling on the shell until it was almost all gone, even though the chick, as mentioned, was dead. This is typical of actions based on instinct; they are continued even though they seem pointless.

Please resist the temptation to help the hatching chick, even if the chick's life is at stake. If you interfere, you will upset the parent bird too much, and she may abandon the entire brood.

Raising the Young

It is just about impossible for a hobby aviculturist to watch the entire process of a parakeet chick's growing up. One would have to peer into the nest box around the clock or install a complicated video camera in a way that would not disturb the birds. Only by looking into the nest box during the mother bird's brief absences can the parakeet owner witness certain moments in the chicks' development. We owe our fairly ex-

tensive knowledge of the life of captive parakeets to the studies of ethologists. For years I, too, have observed the behavior of female parakeets and their offspring and have learned a lot about them. My observations are confirmed by a doctoral thesis written by A. Leuenberger at the University of Bern, Switzerland, and many of the facts cited in the following description are taken from his study.

The Development of Parakeet Chicks

Parakeets are typical nidicolous, or nest-reared birds; the newborn hatchlings are incapable of locomotion at birth. They are also totally naked, blind, and so weak that they cannot even raise their heads—the way other kinds of baby birds do—and crane them toward the mother to beg for food. They are entirely dependent on the mother bird for survival. (Other birds, such as chickens and ducks, are so far developed as newborn chicks that they can follow the mother and look for food immediately after hatching.)

But nidicolous birds, too, develop very quickly once they have hatched. Young parakeets are ready to fly at four weeks, and two months later they are already capable of reproducing. They grow rapidly and reach the adult weight of about thirty grams on the sixteenth or seventeenth day. In the following days they gain a little more but lose this extra weight again by the time they leave the nest box.

The eyes open on the sixth or seventh day. On the seventh day the primary feathers begin to appear, and on the ninth day the tail feathers. The down covering is com-

Breeding Parakeets

plete after ten to eleven days. By the time the birds are four to five weeks old—the point when they are ready to leave the nest box—the large wing feathers have grown three fourths of their full length and the tail feathers two thirds. The young birds are already good fliers. In another seven to ten days the flight feathers are as long as they are going to be.

The coloration of young parakeets before the first molt (the change from juvenile to adult plumage) is not as vivid and brilliant as that of adult birds, and the markings are not as clear. The eyes are completely dark without a light iris. It is not yet possible to sex the young birds by the color of the ceres (the swellings at the base of the nostrils). The change in color of the ceres is gradual and not fully complete until the birds are sexually mature. Up to this point there is no reliable sign by which to sex birds (see page 15).

If you have never seen parakeet chicks just a couple of days old what you see inside the nest box may look odd to you. But it isn't odd at all. The human observer may interpret the typical posture of a chick during its first few days of life as "miserable." The neck is twisted so much that the upper bill or the forehead rests on the floor (see color photo on page 99). The wings hang down on the sides and are slightly bent. In this posture the chick huddles close to its nest mates—with belly, feet, legs, and head on the floor. During this phase the chicks try to stay in constant physical touch with the siblings or the mother and when separated keep turning around in circles and calling until contact is reestablished. The hatchlings of different ages (see page 91) all huddle together with the littlest ones on the bottom

Banding a parakeet chick:
Hold the baby bird in the hollow of your hand and hold the foot gently between thumb and forefinger.

Slide the band first over the two toes pointing forward *and* over the longer one of the two pointing backward;

then slowly push the band
farther back and with the help of a toothpick carefully pull the shorter of the backward-pointing toes out of the band.

This is what the foot looks like when properly banded.

Breeding Parakeets

and the bigger ones on top, neck resting on neck. They maintain these positions even when the mother bird leaves the box, for they have an intense need for body contact. This arrangement also offers warmth, some softness, and an optimal rest position.

By the eighth or ninth day the baby birds are able to hold up their heads and begin to wander around the box and examine their surroundings. They are no longer in constant touch with their siblings but now "examine" them by nibbling at each other. At about three weeks they feed and scratch each other. When the younger chicks beg for food the older ones feed them. At this stage they also display a playful interest in investigating things (droppings). They also nibble on feathers. I have often watched two chicks pick up the same feather, and this would give rise to a delightful game of tug-of-war. Both birds would pull with all their might. When one succeeded in getting the feather away the other would pursue it and the game would start all over.

For the young birds, getting to know their environment and their siblings is important for many reasons. It helps them feel more secure, and it helps strengthen the muscles for flying and eventually leaving the nest. In the course of play with siblings the nestlings practice behavior patterns that will later be crucial for social interaction.

The young parakeets leave their box at about four weeks but are still fed by the parents for a few days. Birds that have already left the nest are sometimes drawn back to the nest by the begging calls of their younger siblings and let themselves be fed along with them. Such birds should not be driven away. It is best to just leave them in the box with the others until they are all ready to go off on their own. As soon as the first nestling leaves the box it is important to place food and water where they are readily found. It is useful to have spray millet and food cups in several spots in the cage or aviary.

One more tip: The keeper should *carefully* peer into the nest box every day and examine the feet and legs of the baby birds. Sometimes feet get sticky with droppings that then harden and hamper the movement of the toes, possibly leading to crippling of the feet. It is important to wipe dirty feet gently with a soft damp cloth or paper towel. Make sure you don't harm feather shafts with blood vessels in them because that would lead to mutilated feathers.

Feeding the Chicks

Like many other habits of parakeets, the mother's way of feeding her chicks is unusual. Already while hatching, the baby birds are able to respond to the mother bird's touch by opening and closing their beaks.

A baby chick's calls and leg kicks are signals for the mother to feed it. She gets up and strokes her bill over the chick's body. To get the chick to assume the feeding position (see illustration on page 95) she pushes her bill against the chick until it lies down on its back. Its bill points straight up, and the chick responds with louder and more urgent cries for food when the mother touches its bill. The mother bird now produces a slimy mixture of saliva and seeds from her crop. (This is not like the "pigeon milk" other kinds of birds feed their young.) She then runs her bill perpendicularly over the chick's bill, and through a rapid vibrating of her head and a shove of her tongue the seeds with the lubricating saliva are slid into the small beak. If the mother interrupts the feeding for a moment the chick raises its head with evident effort and immediately drops it again as soon as the feeding resumes. You might think that the chick would not call so loudly when it is full, but the exact opposite is true. A louder and shriller call means "Please stop feeding me!" The mother strokes and feeds baby birds just a few days old only when they kick and call for food. She does not initiate the feeding as she does with the older chicks (see page 96).

During their first few days the baby birds are fed day and night. The mother spends the entire night with them. It is obviously important that she be able to find her way back to the nest box at dusk and during the night after she has left the box to defecate. I suggest therefore the use of a night light near the cage. This also helps a bird find its way back to the nest if it has been roused by an unfamiliar noise.

The next question for any hobbyist or aviculturist may be what is the best raising feed. In my view, after many years of experience, parakeets do not need any special raising feed if the diet they usually get contains all the necessary nutrients (see page 46). My female parakeets have raised several hundred offspring, all of them birds of excellent health. The prerequisites for raising healthy parakeets are of course not only a proper diet but also optimal living conditions.

Observation of wild parakeets in Australia has shown that the females do not eat anything different while raising their young.

Since commercial parakeet chick feeds do no harm, the choice is up to the individual bird owner.

As the chicks get older the feeding pattern changes. From about the eighth day the nestlings are hardly fed at all at night, even

A parakeet nestling being fed. During the first few days the chicks lie on their backs while being fed. They don't sit up to eat until they are about ten days old.

if they beg for food. The begging behavior of the young birds also changes. After four to six days the chicks no longer lie flat on their backs while being fed. Instead they sit up on their lower backs and call with head raised high. They are not yet strong enough to resist the pressure of the mother's beak when she feeds them and still fall flat on their backs at these times. They start sitting up for the entire feeding from the age of about ten to twelve days. Now they no longer cry louder when full than when hungry (see page 95), but instead turn away and crawl under the mother's wing. The begging behavior becomes discriminating with increasing physical development.

After three weeks the nestlings start wandering about in the nest box and follow the mother, begging for food. They are able to aim their beaks at the mother, and their begging now takes the form of jerking jabs at the food. The mother feeds her three-week-old offspring not only when they beg (see page 95) but when she is ready, i.e., when she returns to the box. To positively urge the young birds to eat, the mother bird runs her bill over their bodies to make them open their bills. If one of them does not open up she turns to the others. The mother bird does most of the feeding, but the male parent also feeds the chicks when they address their begging to him—assuming the mother permits him to enter the box.

Brooding and Defending the Nestlings

Feeding her chicks is not the only job of a mother bird raising a family. She also broods (covers the chicks with her wings to give warmth and body contact) and defends the chicks.

Brooding is especially important during the first few days because parakeet chicks, probably like other nidicolous nestlings, have trouble keeping an even body temperature. If you picture these tiny, naked, blind bits of skin and bone you will realize how much they need their mother's warmth. During the first few days the mother bird

spends almost all her time sitting on the nestlings. She shoves them underneath herself so that they are completely covered. Not until the fourteenth day does she sometimes sit with closed wings next to a chick instead of taking it under her wing. As the nestlings move around more she broods them less, and when the chick that hatched last is sixteen days old she stops sitting on her brood altogether.

If several pairs of birds are breeding in the same aviary the females will defend their broods aggressively (as they do in the wild). Should a strange female peer through the entry hole, the mother bird inside responds instantly and hacks at the intruder. If the latter does not withdraw promptly a fight starts that can lead to serious wounds. This defensiveness about the brood is important because if the mother bird fails to protect her chicks their lives may be in danger. I have seen more than one female intruder kill an entire brood. There are females that go from box to box threatening the established brooding females without wanting to brood themselves. If you have such a troublemaker in your aviary there is only one solution: Remove the bird from the aviary and see if it will start a breeding cycle with a male in a separate cage. I have observed with my birds how two females, each of which had fought to obtain a nest box, proceeded to throw the dead chicks out of the entry hole and then settled down to raise broods of their own in the boxes they had taken by force. Other females attempted to brood with the previous brood of dead chicks still in the box. Needless to say, I removed the dead birds the first chance I had. Such incidents can be prevented only if you check the boxes regularly during the

Breeding Parakeets

breeding period so that you can intervene in time if necessary.

If a Mother Bird Dies

Unfortunately it happens now and then that a mother bird dies while the nestlings are still small. What should you do with the orphaned chicks? There are some male parakeets—though relatively few—that proceed to raise the offspring by themselves. But in most cases the baby birds die unless you can find a foster mother for them. In the care of a female that is raising her own brood at the same time the orphans' chances for survival are quite good. Luckily brooding parakeets accept strange baby chicks even if they are not the same age as the original brood, and a mother bird usually looks after them as though they were her own. It is not hard for a parakeet mother to adjust to having chicks of different ages. If she has, for example, some five-day-old and some three-week-old chicks (her own and strangers) she will feed the younger set day and night and the older ones during the day only (see page 95). Of course to prevent problems you should try to find a female with chicks about the same age as the orphaned ones. If the chicks you add are too much younger than the female's own offspring there is a danger that the younger chicks will not get enough care, because the mothering tasks naturally decrease as the young grow up, and the older the chicks are the more difficult it is for the foster mother to shift gears. (Mr. Leuenberger has studied these behavior patterns in the course of his research at the University of Bern's Ethological Station in Hasli.)

As far as I know, attempts to "hand raise" orphaned parakeets have met with little success. It takes a great deal of time as well as extensive experience with parakeets to stuff into these tiny creatures enough food for them to thrive.

What to Watch Out for after the Chicks Leave the Nest

If your birds breed in an aviary the young will have enough space to train their flight muscles after they leave the nest. Even if the mother bird has already started on another breeding cycle she will not attack her previous offspring in an aviary, something she is quite likely to do in a small cage. If your cage is no bigger than the minimum dimensions given on page 83 it is better to separate the young birds from their parents about two or three days after the young leave the nest. They should be moved to a generously large cage of their own. Make sure they are able to find their food easily (see page 94). As a rule birds of one brood are left together until they are five or six weeks old.

I have never seen any female throw bits of droppings or other dirt out of her box, and I therefore recommend a thorough washing of the box with hot water after each brood leaves. While the chicks still live in the box no cleaning should be attempted. In nature, insects—ants, for instance—sometimes clean the nest cavity.

Under no circumstances should you hang the box back before you are prepared for more offspring from your birds, and I recommend that you not let any female raise more than two broods a year. Otherwise she will grow exhausted and the offspring are likely to be very small and susceptible to disease. Since parakeets living in the wild (see page 112) keep breeding without a break while conditions are optimal (which they usually are in an aviary) it is difficult to keep females from brooding. One way to deal with this is to separate the male and the female after the brooding period and house them in different rooms. If the female has already started to lay eggs again, which is very likely, you wait until all the eggs are laid and then remove the nest box. If you don't wait long enough an egg might remain in the oviduct (egg binding), because the female could not find a suitable place to lay the egg. Egg binding is a very serious condition for the female: Usually she will sit on the ground weak and totally exhausted and hardly moving. If you pick the bird up carefully, hold her belly up, and gently run your finger upward from the vent in the direction of the head you can feel the egg clearly. There is only one way to save the bird: The egg has to be removed immediately. But this has to be left to an expert, preferably an experienced veterinarian, so that the weakened animal is not made to suffer needlessly.

In many cases females lay eggs in the absence of a nest box and even of a partner. These eggs are obviously infertile. Unfortunately there is no easy way to prevent females from laying eggs. Some parakeet owners try to deal with this problem by giving their birds hormone treatments, but these seldom have the desired effect, and in my opinion the harm they do to the birds outweighs the benefits. If a female is no longer going to be used as a breeder, the oviduct can be cut in a simple surgical procedure (see page 75). The only other thing you can do is to watch your birds well to be able to help quickly in case of egg binding.

Apart from separating males from females, there is no effective way to prevent parakeets from breeding. If you don't want your birds to produce offspring you should not keep several pairs together. A single pair is not quite so eager to breed for reasons explained on page 87.

Playing with Colors

Breeding parakeets for specific colors is subject to complicated rules of heredity, and I can explain them here only in broad outline. Anyone who would like to breed for specific colors and wants to avoid haphazard results will have to consult specialized literature. But I can give you a general understanding of how the basic rules of heredity work. When we see a child who has inherited his father's big nose and his mother's blond hair it is obvious that both father and mother pass on traits to their offspring. We conclude that the mother's genes and the father's genes combine to make up the child's genes. This does not mean, of course,

Preening and courtship display. Above: The ▷ female (left) is preening her mate's neck feathers. Below: While singing his courtship song the male (left) is busily tapping the perch with his bill to encourage a receptive mood in the female.

Breeding Parakeets

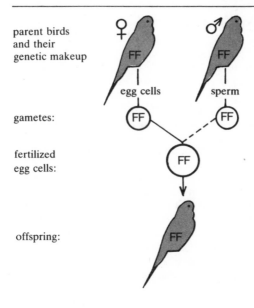

parent birds
and their
genetic makeup

♀ FF   ♂ FF

egg cells   sperm

gametes: FF ... FF

fertilized
egg cells: FF

offspring: FF

How a trait is passed on: If both parents (green) are homozygous, their offspring will also be of a pure green strain (FF = green).

that the child has twice as many genes as each parent. The mother and father each pass on only half of their genes to the child, and the two halves make up one new whole.

The genes that determine what the offspring will look like are located in the nucleus of the male parent's sperm cell and

◁ Wild parakeet female feeding a nestling in a natural nest cavity. For the first eight days the nestlings lie on their backs while being fed.

the female parent's egg cell. These cells are called germ cells or gametes, and each of them contains only half the parent's genes. Within the cell nucleus the genes are located on the chromosomes, which resemble strings with knots in them that form a kind of code. The "knot code words" are the genes. Since both father and mother supply genetic information for all traits, the offspring has a double or diploid set of chromosomes and genes.

What I have just described applies not just to humans but to parakeets as well. The aviculturist's prime interest is of course focused on the genes that determine the coloration and sex of the birds. If both parent birds contributed genes for the identical color, the offspring is pure or homozygous with respect to this trait; i.e., blue plus blue equals blue. If the two parents have different genes for color, on the other hand, the offspring is called heterozygous. The illustration on the left shows in diagram form what happens when a green bird is crossed with a blue one. The gene for color is represented by the letter F, or f (F = green; f = blue). The offspring of such a crossing is not bluish green—there is no such color in parakeets— but the same shade of green as that of the green parent bird. The old saying that appearances deceive applies here as it often does in genetics, for the gene F (green) wins out over the gene f (blue) if both are inherited by the offspring. The trait "blue" does not show up but it can be passed on. If in some future generation a bird ends up with two "f" genes, that bird will be blue. We say that "F" is dominant over "f" and that "f" is recessive. Thus the color of a parakeet does not necessarily tell us what genes that bird possesses.

Breeding Parakeets

parent birds
and their
genetic makeup:

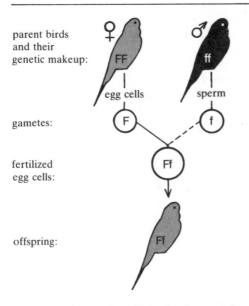

egg cells

sperm

gametes:

fertilized
egg cells:

offspring:

How a trait is passed on: If the female parent has two genes for green (FF) and the male parent has two genes for blue (ff), the offspring will be green but with a recessive gene for blue (Ff).

In parakeets, as in all living creatures, what makes the difference between males and females is that out of all the chromosome pairs one pair is dissimilar. In parakeets, males have many identical pairs plus an xx pair; females have many identical pairs plus an xy pair. The x and y chromosomes are called the sex chromosomes. (In humans, by contrast, the male has the xy chromosomes and the female the xx chromosomes.) To know which sex has the y chromosome is especially important for breeding white and yellow parakeets (see page 104).

What Gives the Feathers Their Colors?

Ordinarily, objects or images look colorful to us because of the color pigments in them. But in certain objects extremely fine structures appear to our eyes as colors. A mass of tiny water drops distributed in a certain way is a case in point; these water drops are perceived by us as a rainbow. In bird feathers both methods of producing color are at work: pigments and structural colors.

A feather has a central shaft, or rachis, and vanes made up of many barbs that branch off from the shaft and interlock with barbules. The shaft provides the feather with rigidity and the vanes give it added surface for flying. The structure of a feather and the cross section of a barb as it appears under a microscope are depicted in the illustration on page 107.

The basic colors of a parakeet's plumage are made up as follows:

White: The horny structure of the feather contains no pigments at all.

Yellow: The outer keratin layer contains yellow pigment; the center contains no pigments.

Blue: The keratin layer is colorless; the air bubbles in the porous zone below the keratin break light down into the rainbow colors. Dark pigments (melanin) in the center absorb all colors except blue; blue is therefore reflected.

Green: The keratin layer contains yellow pigment. The center porous zone creates blue, and yellow plus blue make green.

Black: The keratin layer and the center both contain melanin but there is no yellow pigment.

The four basic colors of parakeets, disregarding black markings, are therefore all

Breeding Parakeets

derived from yellow and black pigments. (The structural color blue appears only if black is present in the central region.) We therefore need symbols only for two hereditary factors. First, there has to be a gene for yellow, which can occur in two states:

- F = yellow pigment is produced;
- f = yellow pigment is not produced.

Secondly, there has to be a gene for black, which can also occur in two states:

- O = black pigment is produced;
- o = black pigment is not produced.

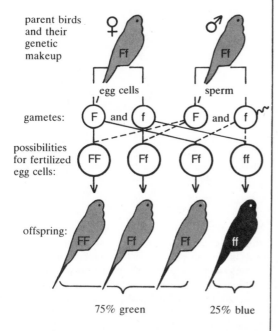

parent birds and their genetic makeup

egg cells   sperm

gametes:

possibilities for fertilized egg cells:

offspring:

75% green   25% blue

How a trait is passed on: Both parents are heterozygous (Ff), meaning green with a recessive gene for blue.

(For accuracy's sake we have to note that there are also intermediary states where black pigment is present in varying concentrations.)

We have already seen that every bird has a double set of genes; the genes for yellow can therefore be in the state "F" or "f." Consequently the trait yellow occurs in one of *three* possible combinations. Any given bird has inherited one of these three combinations from its parents and keeps it for life. The three possibilities are: FF—green; Ff—green, because F is dominant over f; and ff—blue.

If two green parakeets are mated the outcome is quite unpredictable. Two possible results are shown in the diagrams on pages 101 and 103. One more note: The diagram on page 103 shows four offspring. But what can you expect if your bird produced only three eggs? The diagram merely depicts a statistical relationship: 25 percent of the offspring of such matings will have the genes FF, 50 percent will have Ff, and the remaining 25 percent will have ff. In actuality you are not likely to get exactly the predicted percentages. If you want results that accurately reflect the above proportions you have to breed a large number of birds.

What are the Genetics of Albinos and Lutinos?

Albinos are white and lutinos are yellow parakeets with red eyes. To put it in the simplest terms, albinos and lutinos lack the black pigment melanin altogether. This is why these birds do not even have a dark protective layer against light in their eyes, and the red blood shines through. Yellow

Breeding Parakeets

parakeets (lutinos) are descended from the green type; white ones (albinos), from the blue type.

The special thing about the inheritance of the melanin factor is that it is carried on the x chromosome and is therefore sex-linked. The male parakeet has two x chromosomes because his sex chromosomes are xx. The female parakeet's sex chromosomes, however, are xy, and she therefore has only one x chromosome. Whether the gene for melanin pigment is passed on in dominant or recessive form is irrelevant for the female because there is no complementary x gene (the y chromosome is largely deficient in genes). In the two diagrams on the right of this page and on page 105, respectively, two examples of crossing a lutino with a green parakeet are shown. The symbols used are: x = x chromosome with melanin factor (normal); x^0 = x chromosome without melanin factor.

In the first example, depicted in the diagram to the right, a lutino female with the genes x^0 and y is mated with a green male with the genes xx. What is the connection between sex and color in the offspring? All male offspring of such a crossing have normal coloration (green in this case), but they all have a hidden melanin deficiency (they are heterozygous). All female offspring also have normal coloration but they do not have a melanin deficiency even in recessive form. The green males of this generation whose genetic inheritance we now know thanks to our theoretical premises have to be mated with a yellow female if we want to obtain yellow offspring from them.

Because of this complex, sex-linked pattern of inheritance the first yellow parakeets disappeared without leaving behind a yellow strain. Yellow birds turned up once or twice

How sex-linked traits are passed on: Crossing of a lutino female with a green male.

before the turn of the century but the trait did not seem to be passed on to future generations. In the diagram to the right, a lutino female with the genes x^0y is mated with a heterozygous green male (with a recessive trait for yellow) having the genes x^0x. This crossing produces offspring of all possible kinds. The melanin factor occurs in both males and females. If we now want to produce only yellow birds we mate yellow males with yellow females.

Breeding Parakeets

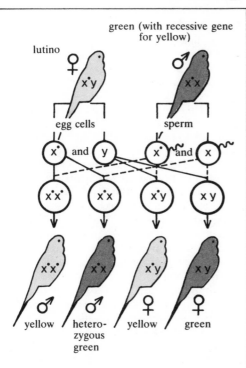

lutino

green (with recessive gene for yellow)

egg cells

sperm

x° and y ⟶ x° and x

$x^{\circ}x^{\circ}$ $x^{\circ}x$ $x^{\circ}y$ xy

$x^{\circ}x^{\circ}$ ♂ yellow

$x^{\circ}x$ ♂ heterozygous green

$x^{\circ}y$ ♀ yellow

xy ♀ green

How sex-linked traits are passed on: Crossing of a lutino female with a heterozygous green male with a recessive gene for yellow.

The pattern is the same for white birds; all we have to do is to replace yellow with white and green with blue in our diagrams.

Things get a little more complicated if we want to cross albinos with green birds or lutinos with blue birds. Now we have to keep track of two genetic factors: the melanin factor, which is located in the x chromosome (sex-linked), and the yellow factor on a "normal" chromosome. To work out the details of such a crossing lies beyond the scope of this book, and I have to refer you to more specialized literature, which "color breeders," especially, should study in detail.

Wild Parakeets in Australia

Much of what we know about parakeets derives from observation of caged birds. But many people who share their lives with one of these "hook bills" are probably curious about the natural conditions and habits of the birds in the wild. I also believe that some knowledge in this area affords you a better understanding of your colorful pet.

The first European to write anything about the parakeet's way of life was John Gould, who published his *Birds of Australia* in 1865. Many bird lovers are thrilled just to leaf through these magnificent books because they contain not only descriptions of many Australian birds but also beautiful engravings and drawings that Gould's wife had made. For a long time Gould's work remained the only source of information on wild parakeets. But today we have not only several good books on the bird life of Australia in which parakeets, too, are discussed at some length, but there is also a remarkably informative film about these small Australian parrots. (The film was made by the filmmakers Arendt and Schweiger, who have also furnished a number of the color photos in this volume.)

Parakeets and Their Relatives

John Gould spent several years traveling all over Australia with his wife. In the course of an expedition into the interior of central Australia he came upon the parakeet, which was given the scientific name *Melopsittacus undulatus Shaw*. The parakeet—or budgerigar, to use its more accurate name—belongs to the family of true parrots, which explains why the parakeet is relatively adept at learning to talk. Parrots make up a distinct group of birds with marked characteristics that make them easy to distinguish from other bird families. One striking trait is the prominent and powerful beak, with the upper mandible protruding and curving down over the lower one. The tip of the upper mandible is notched on the underside, so that parrots can get a firm hold of their food or hang on to branches with their beaks. Of the four toes on each foot two point forward and two backward. The parakeet is the smallest of the flat-tailed parrots (*Platycercini*) and is a genus all to itself. (The *Platycercini* also include birds like the grass parrots, Rosellas, and the New Zealand parrots, which live almost entirely on the ground and are sometimes referred to as the "pheasants" among parrots.)

An explanation of the rules according to which the parakeet was classified with parrots would be too involved here, but the necessity of zoological classification is apparent if we consider the huge number of plants and animals. There has to be some system for us to be sure just what plant or animal someone is talking about. Our system of classification goes back to the Swede Carl von Linné, who made the attempt to catalog the abundance of plant and animal life. This orderly classification (taxonomy) is not an arbitrary result of human thinking, but is based on the assumption that complex living organisms developed in the course of evolution from simpler organisms. The groupings thus also indicate a natural relationship among the members they comprise.

The zoological classification of the parakeet follows:

Class: *Aves* (birds)
Order: *Psittaciformes* (parrots and allies)
Family: *Psittacidae* (parrots)

Wild Parakeets in Australia

Subfamily: *Psittacinae* (true parrots)
Genus group: *Platycercini* (flat-tailed parrots)
Genus: *Melopsittacus*
Species: *undulatus*

The scientific name *Melopsittacus undulatus Shaw* tells us something about the bird and is easy to explain: *Melos* (Greek) means song, *psittacus* (also Greek) means parrot. *Undulatus* is the Latin word for "undulating" and refers to the wavy markings of the plumage. *Shaw* indicates that the English scientist Shaw (in 1794 in his book *Zoology of New Holland*) was the first to describe the parakeet and to give it the name *Melopsittacus undulatus*. In English the bird has two common names: parakeet and budgerigar. Budgerigar is the more specific name because it refers only to *Melopsittacus undulatus* and derives from the name the Australian aborigines gave the bird. They called him "betcherrygah," which says nothing about the bird's nature or appearance but instead means something like "good meal." (Apparently the aborigines liked the taste of parakeet.) "Parakeet" is commonly used in the pet trade to mean "parakeet" and nothing else. However, technically speaking the "parakeets" include other species beside *Melopsittacus undulatus*.

What Wild Parakeets Look Like

A parakeet is somewhat larger than a house sparrow but both birds weigh about the same—slightly over one ounce (30 grams). The wild parakeet is somewhat smaller and lighter than its tame cousin, measuring 6¼ to 8 inches (16–20 cm) from beak to tip of the tail. The wild birds are mostly green or greenish with brown to black stripes on wings and back. Yellow and blue parakeets are occasionally seen in the wild, but they probably do not live long because their conspicuous coloring makes them an easy target for predators. The head is yellow with narrow black stripes, the face (or mask), pale yellow from beak to throat. On the sides the mask is marked off by longish violet "sideburns," below which are three black spots in a line running toward the center of the throat. The tail is very long.

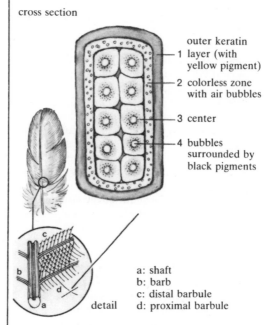

cross section

1 outer keratin layer (with yellow pigment)
2 colorless zone with air bubbles
3 center
4 bubbles surrounded by black pigments

a: shaft
b: barb
c: distal barbule
d: proximal barbule

detail

Structure of a green parakeet feather.

Wild Parakeets in Australia

The round, black pupils of the eyes are surrounded by a thin white iris. The lids shut from below. In adult males the ceres (the swellings at the base of the nostrils) are blue; the ceres of females are brown and often get very dark during the brooding period.

Environment and Distribution

Australia, the homeland of parakeets, is often called a bird paradise. This description seems apt in view of the variety of birds found there and the brightness of their plumage. But the physical conditions to which the creatures of that continent have had to adapt in the course of millions of years are far from heavenly. On the fifth continent, which is the driest of them all, climatic conditions are extreme. A passage from Klaus Immelmann's book *Die Vogelwelt Australiens (The Birds of Australia)* conveys just how extreme, if not hostile, the climate is in the parakeet's range of distribution, i.e., in the interior of Australia: "The tropical north is affected by the northwest monsoon, and after the summer solstice, i.e., in summer and fall, monsoonal rains fall. [Australia lies south of the equator; consequently when it is summer there we have winter, and vice versa.] In the south of the continent the climate is Mediterranean with hot, dry summers and rainy winters. The interior of Australia lies between these two climatic zones and has no regular rainy periods. The precipitation is not linked to any particular season, and sometimes there is no rain for months and even years."

Central Australia—the parakeets' habitat—is a huge, arid region with almost des-ertlike landscapes, tree and brush-dotted steppes, ancient, craggy rock hills, and creeks (which carry water only intermittently). The extreme environmental conditions that prevail in the interior of Australia are hard not only on animals but on people as well. The filmmakers Arendt and Schweiger told me of the extreme discomforts they experienced in filming their extraordinary documentary on parakeets. It takes idealism as well as physical stamina to film parakeets and their offspring at morning and evening temperatures of 100°F (38°C). Because of the heat it was impossible to film at all in the afternoon. Arendt and Schweiger had to make more than one trip to Australia, because the first year they encountered few parakeets and nobody in all of Australia was able to tell them where the birds could be found. The next year they had better luck: They saw huge flocks, probably many thousands of birds that darkened the sky as they passed overhead.

The filmmakers assume that these fluctuations in bird populations are due to extensive dry periods during which thousands of birds die and the survivors move on to areas with more clement conditions. Klaus Immelmann, too, mentions these mass deaths in his book. He tells of a farmer in central Australia who fished five tons of dead parakeets from a single cattle water station, while another farmer removed 60,000 parakeets from a watering place. For the birds who are exhausted by long flights and

A pair of wild parakeets outside their nest cavity. ▷
The male (right) is giving the female food he has regurgitated from his crop.

Wild Parakeets in Australia

weakened by lack of water, the watering stations for cattle are veritable death traps. The watering places on pasture land and near the farms are usually constructed and often have sides that are so steep and high that the birds, weakened from an extensive search for water, cannot climb out with wet feathers. When there are a great many birds they also get in each other's way in trying to take off. During long dry spells the plants and grasses that provide the staple food of parakeets also dry up, of course, and the birds are forced to move on. Living like nomads, they crisscross their huge range, always in search of water and food.

Adaptation to the Environment

Biologists have coined the concept "ecological niche." By this they mean the inter-relationship between the physical parameters of a certain environment and the needs of an animal species, and the form in which the species makes use of the environment. Such a niche is not literally a place but a complex

◁ Parakeets in their native habitat in Australia. Above: This pair has found a hole in a tree that is suitable for breeding. The female is sitting in the entry hole, and the male is on the right. Below: A flock of parakeets drinking and bathing at a water hole.

relationship between the species and the environment. The parakeet has a relatively well-established ecological niche. As you will see in the following sections, the parakeet's way of life and all its behavior patterns are geared to survival in its "hostile" surroundings. For to maintain its ecological niche an animal species has to ensure a good chance of survival and produce a large number of offspring.

How can parakeets suffer such huge losses during the long dry periods without the species dying out? The only way the species can survive is to compensate by reproducing quickly and in great numbers when conditions are favorable. Like almost all the birds found in the dry regions of Australia, parakeets are well adapted to this form of ensuring the survival of the species. Male parakeets are sexually precocious. By the time they are three or four months old their testes are functional. This early sexual development is quite unusual in birds. Young parakeet males have their adult plumage at three months of age; that means they have already completed their juvenile molt. This early maturity means that very young parakeets can reproduce and therefore produce a larger number of offspring. But this by itself would not be enough to produce large populations. It has been observed in caged birds that the testes of the males are active all year round if the birds live in a community and have a chance to brood. In most wild birds the testes shrink after the reproductive cycle is over and no more sperm are produced until the onset of a new mating season is announced by external factors, such as length of day. These signals come early enough for the inactive testes to resume functioning in time. Parakeets, however,

Wild Parakeets in Australia

have to be ready to mate very quickly, almost continuously, in fact, since in central Australia the change from drought to rainfall occurs very quickly and without forewarning. This permanent activity of the testes (as well as the early maturing) is therefore interpreted as a mechanism adaptive to the extreme environmental conditions of the habitat. Parakeets have to start raising their young as soon as there is enough water and food after the rains.

Ornithologists were therefore much taken aback when not all wild parakeets turned out to have permanently active testes. We

During copulation the parakeet male spreads one wing over the female.

have already mentioned that the range of parakeets extends all over central Australia. But these birds are also found near the coast in the northwest and in the central southern areas. In some regions parakeets were found with cyclical activity of the testes like those of many of our wild birds. This means that the climatic conditions where these parakeets lived must be such that the birds can take their time reproducing. Males with testes active throughout the year, rather than cyclically, were found where it was important to the birds' survival to reproduce quickly. (Thus, it seems, the house of science is in order once again.)

But this is not the end of the adaptive mechanism. Parallel to the early maturing of the testes, courtship behavior starts extremely early among parakeets. The males seek out partners even before reaching sexual maturity. The male takes the initiative (see page 86) although the final choice is the female's, and the female responds to the courting of an adolescent male with mutual scratching and nibbling of the plumage.

Many of the birds are thus already bonded by the time they reach sexual maturity. They do not then choose new partners after every brood but remain faithful to the mate over a period of time (see page 85). This early pairing and the bonding to *one* partner make it possible for wild parakeets to mate immediately when the conditions are right so there is no loss of time.

Wild Parakeets' Brooding

Another factor in ensuring a high birth rate is the large number of eggs (4 to 8) in a clutch. If the conditions are favorable one

Wild Parakeets in Australia

brood follows after another. The females lay their eggs in suitable holes in trees without using any nesting materials. It would seem that the limited number of trees would be a problem, but this is not the case. If the females do not find enough trees they will brood in holes in the ground or in any other cavity they can find. Arendt and Schweiger told me that they saw females sitting on eggs in cavities where there was hardly room for them to turn around. It is hard to imagine how these birds manage to raise their young in such narrow quarters.

Normally the females find holes in old or dead trees, hardly ever in young ones. They prefer trees standing close to creeks or in floodplains with some water. The inside of the hole is left as it is. Arendt and Schweiger were able to observe that the bottom usually consisted of soft, decayed wood that was slightly moist from the chicks' droppings. Insects (ants, for instance) and their larvae keep the cavity clean.

The females whittle the entry holes with their beaks to make them round or oval and to create an opening about 1¼ to 2½ inches (3–6 cm) across. This size is ideal. If the opening is smaller parakeets have trouble squeezing through, and if it is larger, predators, competitors for the nest site, and nest robbers would endanger eggs and chicks. It is amazing how deep some of the holes are. The biologist Edmund Wyndham found some where the distance between entry hole and the bottom was three feet. It is hard to imagine how the fledglings manage to get out of such a hole. Observation has shown that domesticated parakeets often choose one nesting box over another on the basis of where the perch is located in relation to the entry hole. Boxes with the perch directly under the hole are preferred. Wild parakeets show no such preference. Branches that are in the way are simply gnawed off. A number of birds can nest in the same tree at the same time without interfering with each other. The distance between nesting holes varies but was always over three feet in observed colonies.

Hatching and Raising the Young

As far as I know no one has yet actually seen a wild parakeet hatchling emerge from an egg. Even Arendt and Schweiger missed this. They were always too late and would find the empty shell with the naked chick already outside. But from what was left of the shell I assume that the hatching of wild birds is similar to that of domesticated ones. Nor did the two filmmakers see the parakeet mother remove the egg shell as I have seen my birds do in my aviary. The reason may simply be that individual birds act somewhat differently or, possibly, that there is a real disparity in behavior between wild and domesticated birds. It would take more systematic observation to make any conclusive statement. According to Arendt and Schweiger the air in the nesting cavities is very hot but also extremely dry. This dryness may possibly affect the hatching process. As already described on page 90, the chick pecks a small hole into the shell from the inside with its egg tooth. Then it rotates a little, pecks again, and gradually succeeds in making a thin crack. This rotating motion within the egg becomes more difficult or impossible if the embryo sticks to the egg membranes because it is too dry. The chick then keeps working away at the same spot, making a hole rather than a crack in the shell. Once in this situation the chick could not break out of the egg unless the mother helped by enlarging the hole. Ornithologists have observed in other species of birds that the degree of humidity affects the hatching process. Amelie Koehler, a biologist, observed a falcon female enlarge the peck hole of a chick that was stuck inside its shell. When she sprayed some water on the rest of the eggs these chicks hatched normally.

Parakeet chicks that need assistance to hatch are just as vigorous and viable as those that make it on their own. I have never seen any of them more frail than its siblings, let alone die of weakness. Still, without the mother's help these chicks would die, which would in the long run have a negative effect on the population rate. If the low humidity in the parakeet's native habitat can actually cause embryos to get stuck inside their shells, then the female's assistance during the hatching of her young would be one more adaptive mechanism—in addition to numerous broods per year, large clutches, and early sexual maturity—to the harsh environmental conditions of central Australia.

To my knowledge there are no scientific studies, apart from the Arendt and Schweiger film, about the behavior of nestlings and their parents. But I have the impression that there are no significant differences in this respect between wild and domesticated birds. In the wild, too, as in our aviaries, the baby birds are fed lying on their backs for the first few days. As soon as the neck muscles are strong enough, the young birds begin to raise their heads toward the mother. The begging behavior is also simi-

A wild parakeet female feeding her chicks in the nest cavity.

lar, and the need for physical contact is just as obvious. Like the birds in our nest boxes, wild parakeet siblings are crowded together in the nest cavity, the youngest on the bottom, the bigger ones on top, neck resting on neck. How the birds keep from overheating and manage to breathe lying on top of each other like this at 110°F (43°C) is beyond my comprehension, but it seems that wild parakeets thrive better in high temperatures than low ones, for when it is cold there are considerable losses.

While the female broods the male feeds her, because she leaves the nest only occasionally while the nestlings are small. (The same is true of the birds in our aviaries; see page 88.) The parent birds feed their young the same grass seeds they eat themselves (see Feeding, page 118). It would make little biological sense for wild parakeets to spe-

Wild Parakeets in Australia

cialize in specific kinds of grasses or a special rearing diet for their young. On the contrary, this would reduce the chances of survival, because specific plants are available only at certain times of the year, and parakeets don't take time of year into consideration for mating (see page 111). Here is one point in which wild parakeets differ from domesticated ones: The young are fed by their parents no longer than two days after leaving the nest. A plausible reason for this would be that the parent birds want to conserve their energies for the next brood.

Just how significant the losses among the young are before they reach independence (as well as the reasons for the losses) has been studied in several selected sites in the south and southeast of Australia. To do this the breeding success of the birds had to be watched. (By breeding success we mean the survival rate of the eggs during incubation and of the nestlings before they leave the nest.) Since parakeets often nest in tall eucalyptus trees, this was quite an undertaking. The observers had to climb the trees and count the nestlings in the holes without disturbing them. But they used a clever method: They held a mirror inside the entry hole and shone a flashlight down into the hole. This way they could count eggs and hatchlings. It takes some mathematics to arrive at an exact scientific analysis of the data, and a full explanation would lead us too far afield. I will therefore simply summarize the results: In 25 percent of the cases the female abandoned the nest before the eggs hatched; 8 percent of the nests were vandalized, presumably by predators; and 20 percent of the eggs did not hatch because they were infertile or because the embryo died. Combining all the significant factors

and taking specific conditions into account, scientists come up with a breeding success of 63 percent. (The percentage figures cannot simply be added to arrive at a correct mathematical analysis.) There is no scientific standard to tell whether this figure is high or low. But if we consider the extreme environment in which the birds live, we can say unscientifically that a success rate of 63 percent seems quite respectable.

The Parakeet's Enemies

In spite of what seems from our human perspective a remarkable adaptability to the environment, wild parakeet parents have a hard time raising their young to adulthood. Like all animals in the wild they face many predators and competitors for the nest sites. In his doctoral thesis on the ecology of parakeets, Edmund Wyndham vividly describes who these enemies are and how they threaten the birds. He saw, for instance, how a female that had just laid her first eggs was driven from her nest by an Australian swift. (I was surprised to learn this, since the swift is not much larger than a parakeet, and the females in our aviaries aggressively defend their eggs and nestlings against intruders.) The swift proceeded to lay her eggs in the cavity, and the parakeet female never came back.

Among the rivals for nesting sites count the owlet nightjar, a plump, insect-eating bird about 7½ to 11 inches (19–28 cm) long that is widely distributed in Australia. This bird, too, has been observed routing a parakeet female from her nest. The owlet nightjar is the subject of many interesting stories and legends, one of which follows: The

Wild Parakeets in Australia

tribes of southwest Australia believed that kangaroos were originally created blind and without sense of taste, so that they were an easy prey to hunt. According to the natives it was the nightjar, a bird that looks somewhat like a small owl, that gave the kangaroo the senses it lacked.

But back to parakeets. When the chicks get a little older they are exposed to new dangers. At about three or four weeks they stick their heads out of the entry hole and beg loudly for food. This can be fatal because their noise attracts dangerous birds, such as the pied butcherbird, which kills the exposed begging nestlings, pulls them out of the hole, and eats them.

Because of its climate and large desertlike areas, Australia is ideal for reptiles. There are probably more snakes in Australia than anywhere else, so it is not surprising that snakes take their toll of brooding birds. (I have already mentioned on page 115 what percentages of young birds are killed by competitors and nest robbers.)

The parakeet is designed to help overcome the hardships of the Australian environment. Both juvenile and adult birds have in their favor their greenish coloration, which serves as camouflage; the birds are practically invisible in the shadows of tall trees. Parakeets are also acrobatic and fast fliers. In his years of studying the birds Wyndham only once saw a slightly wounded parakeet caught in flight. In twelve other incidents observed by Wyndham the parakeets always escaped their enemies, even though these included skilled fliers like the peregrine falcon that has specialized in flying prey. The falcons predominantly attack parakeets that are resting on a branch, flying alone, or feeding on the ground. When the parakeets notice a raptor they emit an alarm call and immediately fly off. Because of their skill in abruptly changing directions while flying fast they usually escape unscathed.

Chances of being captured by a peregrine falcon are even slimmer when parakeets fly in flocks. Apparently the predators have trouble focusing on one bird in a dense flock and find it hard to pick out prey to pounce on. Traveling in flocks has other advantages for parakeets, which we will discuss in the next section.

Life in a Flock

Many species of animals form groups beyond the ties of pair and family; a larger number of individuals band together either temporarily or permanently in herds or flocks. Within the groups of many of these species there are fights over feeding grounds, the best territory, or a favored female. But these contests hardly ever end

Our parakeets pick food kernels and gravel off the cage or aviary floor with rapid pecking motions; their wild cousins find their food almost exclusively on the ground.

Wild Parakeets in Australia

fatally, because they are conducted according to strict rules. Tournament rules are found not only among humans but in the animal kingdom as well. In the course of these contests some individuals in the group develop greater strength and authority. They rank at the top of the group, and a hierarchy, or what in chickens is called a "pecking order," gets established.

No such ranking order has been observed in wild parakeets. All the members of the flock seem to be equal, and aggressive behavior is rare. Only the nest cavity is defended to a distance of a few yards. My observations of the birds in my aviary indicate that domesticated parakeets behave similarly, even though some authors believe that they have found evidence of a ranking order in captive parakeets. I believe that what these authors report is closely connected to the conditions under which the observed birds live. In birds that live in cages the daily rhythm of the individuals differs and many normal patterns of behavior are suppressed. Not having a daily food search, crowding on perches, and limited opportunity for exercise may lead to greater and more frequent aggression, creating the impression of a ranking order within the group. The social structure of parakeets is the flock, and within the flock there is no ranking order.

The advantages of living together in a flock are obvious. A flock can find food sources more easily, and mutual warning calls serve as protection against predators. If there is any danger around, a characteristic alarm is sounded, and the flock take off instantly. This penetrating sound of alarm is heard especially when the birds are disturbed while feeding.

Parakeets groom each other's plumage lovingly and at great length, especially in the places a bird cannot reach with its own beak.

Huge flocks of several thousand birds descend onto the open grasslands in the early morning and late afternoon to feed. Smaller flocks can be seen in wooded areas. While the birds feed on the ground the flock sometimes changes its formation. Birds that were earlier seen at the tail end of the flock fly over the others and settle down at the head. The grouping within the flock does not reflect age or sex. Young birds just out of the nest mingle with older ones, and males and females are represented in more or less equal numbers.

If some birds flying overhead see others feeding they join in so that the flock keeps growing. This behavior can also be seen in domesticated parakeets. If even a single bird starts to search for seeds on the ground, the others immediately follow suit.

Parakeets hardly ever do anything individually; they do almost everything in the company of others. After their morning meal, which each bird looks for independently, they usually retire to the cool shade of trees along the creeks. If it gets hotter than 95°F (35°C) they spread their wings slightly and pant with open beak. This is how they attempt to stay cool. During the midday heat they have a siesta. Only rarely does one see a pair engaged in mutual preening or hear a bird chirp to itself. The peace is disturbed only if a neighbor gets too close on the perch. The offended one responds by drawing itself up to its full height: The neck stretches, the joints of toes and feet straighten, and the head feathers are raised to intimidate the offender (see illustration on page 125). If the latter does not retreat instantly it is hacked at, although—as mentioned earlier—fights are extremely rare in a flock of parakeets.

Feeding and Food

Parakeets are very quiet when feeding. They climb onto the plant and peel the seeds with their beaks or pick up ripe seeds from the ground. Most of the seeds they eat are hard and ripe. There is only one plant of which they prefer the soft, unripe seeds, and there is no indication that parakeets seek out soft, unripe seeds (which are more easily digestible) for their young.

The diet of wild parakeets includes the seeds of twenty-one species of plants—a remarkable variety. Most of these plants are grasses. To list all these plants would be too

complicated, especially since the Latin names would have to be given, because many of the species are rare or nonexistent here. I want to mention only the four most important forage plants. They are *Astrepla lappacea*, *A. pectinata*, *Atriplex angulata*, and *Boerhavia diffusa*.

Parakeets are not fussy; they make do with whatever plants are available after a rainy spell. (They have never been observed eating insects or other animal food.) This helps them survive in drought-stricken areas. Of course there are gourmets among them who have a special liking for certain plants if available. One bird has been observed, for instance, who liked to eat plants of the *Astrepla* genus while most of the flock was eating *Boerhavia* and *Panicum* plants.

Wild parakeets drinking at a watering place.

For parakeets, as for all animals living in a desertlike environment, finding water is a major problem. In dry years thousands of birds may gather around one watering place no matter how shallow it may be. The flocks usually drink between their morning feeding and their siesta and again in the late afternoon. But this daily rhythm is not always predictable; it also depends on the temperature. In cooler weather the birds don't drink regularly, and on some days they don't visit a watering place at all. Studies have shown that at a temperature of 68°F (20°C) and a humidity of 30 percent wild parakeets can survive up to thirty days without drinking any water at all. (Don't try this experiment on your caged bird!) In the extreme temperatures of its native habitat a wild parakeet must use sparingly whatever water is available. It is not surprising then that these birds remain almost motionless during the midday heat. Movement increases the oxygen consumption of an organism, lung activity increases, and more body fluid evaporates. Resting prevents water loss the birds cannot afford. This is one more example of how the behavior patterns of parakeets reflect their physical needs and thus enable the birds to survive in their Australian homeland.

The Behavior of Parakeets

Understanding Parakeets

Ever since Professor Konrad Lorenz's wonderful, nontechnical books based on his intensive observation of animal behavior many parakeet owners have wanted to learn as much as possible about the behavior of their birds. Careful scientific studies have provided insight into some behavior patterns of parakeets, and observation of the birds in their Australian habitat has yielded further clues. Last but not least, the decades of experience of keepers and breeders of parakeets have contributed to our knowledge. This chapter on parakeet behavior is meant to enable the parakeet fancier—and especially keepers and breeders—to understand parakeets better and to aid in creating an environment that does justice to these sociable, "intelligent," and charming creatures.

But remember in reading the following pages that no living creature, especially one as highly developed as the parakeet, always conforms to the typical behavior of its species. And our birds that have lived for generations so far from their original habitat and under totally different conditions show deviations from their natural behavior patterns.

If your bird does not exactly fit the descriptions that follow, this may be because of different living conditions, the particular personality of your parakeet, or perhaps some degeneration, which is not necessarily to be viewed negatively. The bird has simply adjusted to living under the care of humans.

Social Behavior

A bird that lives with many others of its kind in a flock and would probably not survive long in nature as a loner has to be able from birth to get along peacefully with its fellows. It takes a number of innate differentiated forms of expression for birds to live together in a flock and to guarantee smooth natural social interactions. All social behavior is involved here, i.e., all communication with fellow members whether it be expressed by voice, posture, or by a sequence of actions. These forms of behavior are intelligible to all members of the flock as well as to the sexual partner. The latter point is especially important with parakeets because these birds tend to live monogamously. Among parakeets everything from courtship and mating to the selection of nesting sites, raising young and introducing juvenile birds into the flock, as well as all interaction within the flock, including even aggression, is regulated by universally understood patterns of behavior that are therefore typical of the species.

Human beings can express their feelings and intentions by means of a language that they have learned when young and that they keep expanding with the aid of their brains. Parakeets, too, can learn, but most of their means of communication are inborn.

As already mentioned, movement, posture, and vocal utterance are the signals that either singly or in combination affect the actions and the inner state of other birds; these signals can have a soothing or an agitating effect. It is easy to see, for instance, the calming effect of mutual scratching of the head.

The Behavior of Parakeets

Head Scratching

If you have a pair or a small flock of parakeets in your aviary you will no doubt have observed two birds taking turns scratching each other's head (see illustration on page 12 and color photo on back cover). One of the birds sits erect and gently works over the head and neck region of the partner who deliberately turns and offers places with slightly ruffled plumage for scratching. Sometimes the bird who is having its head scratched jerks back suddenly with a short cry although clearly having a good time. Perhaps the eager partner has touched a tender spot, such as a feather that is just growing in and is still sheathed. The grooming is interrupted briefly but usually resumed shortly in a less sensitive spot. Occasionally an irritating move results in the switching of roles or even in the termination of mutual preening, but I have never seen two birds fight after mutual head scratching, which suggests that this activity is soothing to both parties.

One thing that mutual head grooming indicates is that strong bonding has taken place. Only parakeets that have accepted each other as partners engage in this gesture. Its soothing effect probably arises in part from the sense of contentment the birds feel because each is close to its chosen companion rather than alone. In parakeets that live in captivity it often makes little difference whether two birds are a "true" pair, i.e., birds belonging to opposite sexes, or whether they are both of the same sex with one of them acting the male part and the other the female part (see page 8). If a bird who is not in the mood to have its head scratched simply moves away or turns briefly to its partner in a threatening way with open bill. This is usually enough to discourage the other bird, who then often proceeds to groom itself or starts gnawing on some object.

Mutual head grooming also has a useful hygienic function. To scratch, a parakeet can reach head and neck with its feet, but a partner can do a much better job in smoothing down the small contour feathers, removing dust particles and, if there are any, parasites. A bird that is kept singly has to make do with its feet for keeping head and neck plumage in good order, or the bird can rub its head against the cage bars. If the bird is interested in more than hygiene and if you have won its full confidence, the bird may entrust you with the role of surrogate partner. One day your pet will stretch its head and neck toward you with slightly raised feathers while sitting somewhat hunched. What the bird is communicating to you is: "Please scratch my head." Now you must run your little finger very gently over the bird's head and neck against the lie of the feathers and continue to do so as long as the bird sits still and enjoys it. And give your bird a chance to return the service to fill the need to reciprocate the pleasure you have given. Take the bird on your hand and leave your pet the choice whether it wants to groom the hair on your arm or your head or chew on your cheek or earlobe. You will soon feel that the grooming administered to you with great seriousness and absorption is not a gentle stroking but more like a pinch massage.

The Behavior of Parakeets

Feeding the Partner

Normally the only birds that beg for food are young birds still under parental care. But occasionally females will beg food from males. These females repeatedly open their bills and emit sharp but not very loud chirps that resemble the begging calls of young birds. I have never seen a male begging from a female. Begging and feeding seem to strengthen the bond between two partners the way mutual head scratching does. Both types of behavior are practiced outside the mating and breeding cycle. While the birds are raising young the male *always* brings food to the female (see Feeding the Chicks, page 94). During the courtship period however (see page 86), or when the male is feeding the female to strengthen pair bonding, there is often no real passing of food; the birds are only rubbing bills (see illustration on page 35). In these situations the male does not bring up food from his crop but only acts as if he wants to feed his mate.

Courtship

Courtship comprises a whole complex of behavior patterns that ultimately lead to the mating of two birds (see Courtship and Mating, page 86). The parakeet male has to do a lot of wooing before he wins his mate. In a flock of birds both the males and the females are free to choose partners on the basis of individual preference. If a bird is kept singly and the owner introduces a new bird of the opposite sex, the course toward pair bonding progresses from mutual tolerance to gradual acquaintance to overtures of greater closeness on the part of the male to a generally positive response of the female and, with some luck, finally to actual mating. But not all couples who were arbitrarily introduced to each other oblige by mating. Many bird couples exist in harmony for years and go through many phases of courtship behavior but never reach the natural goal of producing young because

In the course of courtship display the male parakeet (left) taps his bill against the female's repeatedly and with growing excitement.

they fail to get into breeding condition. Maybe the problem is the absence of nest boxes or the lack of stimulation through other birds that are going through the mating cycle (see page 87).

Whether living in a flock or with his mate only, a male parakeet tries to rouse the female's mating instinct. He moves as close to the chosen female as he can and tries to draw her attention to him with a soft chirping, his

The Behavior of Parakeets

courtship song. The feathers on his head and throat are slightly puffed up, and he keeps moving a couple of inches away from the female and then back again, tapping her repeatedly with his bill (see illustration on page 122).

His excitement is evident in his rapid bowing before the female. The pupils of his eyes are contracted so much that the white irises become clearly visible. He also tries to feed her (see page 86 for courtship feeding and also the illustration on page 35).

Mutual grooming of the head feathers is also part of courtship behavior. But here it is usually the male who offers the service (see Head Scratching on page 121). If the female is not interested in the male's overtures she keeps edging away from him, displays her threatening gesture, and—if he is too forward—hacks at him until he finally gives up. But quite often a female changes her mind and gives in if he courts her persistently. If not, both birds try to find different partners.

Courtship displays are repeated over and over. The male feeds the female more and more frequently to put her in a peaceful and agreeable mood. When his wooing is finally successful the female adopts the typical mating position (see illustration on page 87). The head is thrown back, the feathers on the head are somewhat puffed up, and the tail feathers point upward. The male approaches her from the side and briefly puts one foot on the female's back. Finally he mounts her and lowers his tail end on top of the female's vent. During copulation, which lasts only a few seconds, he spreads one wing over the female (see color photo on page 127). Sometimes the male also grabs hold of the female's bill with his own

to help him stay balanced (see page 87).

I have said repeatedly that a singly-kept parakeet is deprived of the life parakeets are meant to live. Only someone who has witnessed the tender billing and cooing of a parakeet pair, the persistent efforts that precede mutual affection, and the rituals of courtship and mating can truly appreciate how desperately a single bird seeks ways that allow expression of its unfulfilled instinctual life. Birds either lose their liveliness, seek consolation in eating, and become uninterested, turning into living ornaments, or they form an attachment to a human, trying to find some form of expression for their natural need to reproduce. Thousands of male parakeets desperately turn to courting shiny objects. Mirrors have thus become the prime accessory bird fanciers buy for their parakeets, because they believe that these objects satisfy the male bird's innate need for executing courtship displays. But a mirror provides no real relief, because in natural courtship behavior the action shifts back and forth between the two partners and normally leads to the act of mating. Obviously not every courtship display leads to copulation (see page 122), but the male always evokes responses characteristic of the species, and quite frequently his efforts in fact lead to success. The mirror offers no such rewards, and the misguided courtship behavior the mirror evokes can result in abnormalities in reproductive behavior after even a few months. Therefore anyone who wants at some point to relieve a parakeet's loneliness by introducing a female bird and who would enjoy watching a family of birds should not risk disturbing the bird's natural mating behavior and should therefore refrain from buying a mirror.

The Behavior of Parakeets

Aggressive Behavior

Parakeets are by nature peaceful birds and are not equipped with features that can serve as weapons, such as the sharp beaks of predator birds. A parakeet tries to flee from its enemy; it never defends itself by fighting. Within the flock there are no contests over rank as they occur in many other bird associations. Nevertheless, no community of animals can get along without some potential form of aggression to secure certain rights, in keeping rivals at bay when courting a mate, and in defending a site for rearing young. If we recall the conditions under which parakeets live in their native Australia, the hasty activity during breeding time, the exertions of the parent birds while rearing their young, and the restless search for food and water in their nomadic wanderings, we can easily see why the birds of this species do not want to waste strength on individual conflicts. Aggression is expressed primarily through threatening behavior, and the offender's compliant response usually settles the matter quickly.

Body posture and vocal utterance are used by parakeets to express displeasure. Tense stance combined with flattened plumage, raised body, stretched spine, and head cocked at the offending bird warn the culprit to watch its step. This signal is reinforced by a threatening call. To further intimidate an opponent a parakeet tries to make itself appear taller by straightening the joints of its feet and by making threatening hacking gestures with open beak. The bird that evoked the aggressive response usually flies away. But in certain situations it responds to this bullying by throwing back its head and sounding a warning call of its own.

As far as I know real fights leading to serious injuries have been observed only in captive parakeets. Females are usually more combative than males, but if an actual fight develops, both sexes make use of the same methods: One bird approaches the other head-on and tries to pull its opponent's feathers or bite its feet. The one under attack tries to parry with its beak, and a violent beak duel ensues until one of the contestants turns to flee. If the two birds are an equal match, it sometimes happens that one of them suddenly plants its foot against its opponent's chest with wide open beak and flattened feather (see illustration on page 125). The victor quite often pursues its beaten enemy for a while after the battle is over. Only rarely, however, have I observed a bird attacking another in midair and continuing the fight on the ground.

There is no evidence thus far that parakeets have an aggression-inhibiting mechanism such as the one we are familiar with in dogs. If two dogs fight, the loser exposes its throat, the most vulnerable part of its body. This so-called submission gesture, in which the loser throws itself totally at the mercy of its enemy, has the effect of inhibiting aggressive behavior in the stronger dog. In my view no comparable submission gesture exists among parakeets. But there have to be other behavior patterns that block aggressions in a flock, because juvenile birds (fledglings) evoke threatening gestures less than older birds. It has been suggested that the imperfect physical coordination of fledglings has an aggression-inhibiting effect on the adults.

This description of aggressive behavior and actual fights gives rise to the question of how we as bird keepers can prevent actual

The Behavior of Parakeets

Threatening gesture when two birds are an equal match for each other: The threatening bird, with bill wide open, is planting its foot on its opponent's chest.

combat. There is little cause for concern where a pair have adjusted to each other, because males hardly ever attack females. In a heterosexual pair the female controls how close or distant she wants to be and the male tends to go out of his way to accommodate his partner. Fights can arise if we inadvertently or thoughtlessly add a second female to an established pair. The male rarely pays special attention to the new female (though it sometimes looks as though he'd like to), but a situation of rivalry has nevertheless been created, and serious contests between the females follow. Usually one of the two females prevails and then tries to bite her rival viciously. Even in a large aviary or in free flight in the room she will continue to attack her competitor. The only solution is to separate the birds immediately or to find a male for the second female.

If you keep a small flock of parakeets in an aviary you can avoid fights only if there are not too many birds for the size and arrangement of the available space. The aviary has to have enough flight space for all birds, and each bird should have a small corner and a perch of its own. It is important that there be more males than females to avoid fights arising from rivalry. Every potential pair should have the choice between two equally desirable nest boxes (see page 84).

Vocal Utterances

Compared to other birds parakeets are not very inventive in their vocal utterances; they produce nothing like the melodious songs of our native songbirds. One important communication for birds living in a flock is the *distance call*, perhaps more correctly described as "contact" call, because it helps the birds stay in touch with each other. Birds also recognize each other individually by this call, because each parakeet has a slightly different version. The distance call also makes it possible for a bird to locate its fellows even when they are out of sight.

125

The Behavior of Parakeets

Because of this acoustic signal each bird knows just where the others are even when the flock is somewhat dispersed. Caged birds also produce the distance call. If two parakeets that are used to each other are separated, they start calling for each other with a persistence that can be nerve-racking. I experienced this one day when one partner of a tame pair escaped. Although both birds were exceptionally trusting and affectionate, I was unable to console the one that was left. He continued his long and penetrating calls for three days until, luckily, the missing bird was returned to me. This is one of the incidents that convinced me that, no matter how tame a parakeet may be, its need for a companion of the same species can never be fully satisfied by a human being.

The *alarm call* is quite different from the distance or contact call. Parakeets warn the flock with this short and shrill call when they spot a bird of prey or some other danger. Usually this call is accompanied by instant flight. Caged birds, too, can produce this sound if they are alarmed by a large bird that is flying by close to the window or over the aviary or if an unusual dangerous-sounding noise frightens them.

At dusk, about a quarter of an hour before dark and after the flock has gathered in the tops of trees, a call sounding something like "*eeaye*" can be heard, followed by a soft chirping with which the birds apparently murmur themselves to sleep. In aviaries and cages this soft chirping is also produced by parakeets as they settle down for the night. In nature it probably provides a feeling of closeness in the flock, just as the distance call does during the day.

The soft, twittering *courtship song* of male parakeets is a sound often heard during the courtship display (see page 86).

Parakeets also use vocal utterances to express moods. A soft chirping similar to that preceding sleep at night suggests relaxed contentment. At the other end of the scale are the piercing shrieks that parakeets produce when agitated. This racket is familiar to any parakeet keeper. Even singly-kept birds are very vocal in announcing their displeasure, the cause of which is often quite obscure to humans.

Comfort Movements

Comfort behavior includes all grooming activity, such as preening, scratching, and bathing; all movements that stimulate the metabolic functioning, such as yawning and stretching wings or legs; and behavior patterns that serve to equalize temperature fluctuations and provide a balance of activity and rest.

During copulation the parakeet male wraps one ▷ wing around the female, a form of behavior that so far seems to be unique among birds.

The Behavior of Parakeets

Grooming

Preening: A parakeet spends several hours a day preening its plumage. Obviously it is not grooming itself constantly, but almost any activity, whether it be feeding, sleeping, or doing something with a partner, is concluded with a few minutes of preening. The care of feathers is important because only a bird whose plumage is always smooth, clean, and lightly oiled is uninterruptedly in command of its full flying powers. When preening itself a bird runs its feathers through its bill one at a time, smoothing each and ridding each of even the minutest dirt particles and of tiny flakes that are left from the sheaths of new feathers. With acrobatic skill parakeets twist and turn to run even the long tail and flight feathers through the bill (see color photos on back cover). The smaller contour feathers are groomed in what often looks like frantic activity; breast, belly, legs, underside of wings, and back all get their turn. Even the naked feet and toes are attended to with the beak and all dirt and skin particles removed. Only the head and neck are worked over with the toes.

◁ A flock of parakeets in Australia. The birds fly long and fast as they roam across the steppes and semi-deserts of their native continent in search of food and water.

In contrast to many larger parrots, parakeets have an oil gland (also called preen gland or uropygial gland). This gland, which consists of a ring-shaped skin fold containing a fatty substance, is located under the feathers on the lower back just above the spot where the tail feathers grow. When preening itself the parakeet frequently rubs its head over this gland, thereby presumably activating the gland and at the same time oiling the head feathers. The bird also removes fat with its bill and then distributes the fat evenly over individual feathers as well as over the feet and toes. This coating keeps the plumage from getting soaked in the rain or during a quick bath. The water cannot penetrate into the feathers but quickly runs off the smooth surface. The oil also protects the feathers from drying out in heat and wind.

Scratching: Parakeets use one method for scratching the head and another method for scratching the sides of the posterior body. Barbara Brockway, an American biologist, found that the way parakeets scratch their sides seems to be unique among birds. To scratch its side the parakeet uses the joint between the tarsometatarsus and the toes as well as the outer sides of the two toes pointing forward. The same parts of the foot—instead of the claws—are used for scratching around the vent to avoid irritating this sensitive area. To scratch its head, however, the parakeet uses the longest toe and its claw, raising the leg under the wing or from behind the wing to reach up to the head (see illustration on page 130). Scratching is part of grooming; it is a preliminary cleaning that precedes the more thorough preening with the bill.

The Behavior of Parakeets

Birds scratch more than usual during molt, presumably because they itch as new feathers grow in and because the feather sheaths are most easily removed through scratching, especially in places the bill cannot reach. Birds also scratch noticeably more when they are infested with pests, such as mites.

If a parakeet's vent region is very dirty the bird's keeper will notice this because of increased scratching. The keeper should then check to see if the vent is red or inflamed. If this is the case the bird's diet may be causing the problem, or the bird may be suffering from an illness.

Head rubbing or head chafing: I have seen this only rarely in my birds, but many writers on parakeets report that these birds often chafe their heads against objects inside the cage or against the cage bars. This is clearly a form of scratching and, because it affects a relatively large area all at once, it also relieves itching, especially the itching caused by mites.

Care of the Bill: Parakeets dispose of bits of leftover food and of dirt by whetting their bills on a perch, the cage grating, or a branch. This whetting can be observed almost every time after a bird eats, even if there is no visible trace of food left on the bill. If mere rubbing does not do the job, chaff or husks that are stuck are removed with the foot.

Working with the bill is an important part of a parakeet's bill care. A parakeet therefore needs more activity for its bill than merely hulling seed kernels. In its native habitat the parakeet uses its bill extensively as a tool for climbing feats, both head up and head down, when inspecting rough tree trunks and branches for usable nest holes.

The bill provides an indispensable hold both in negotiating difficult climbing passages and in excited courtship displays. By whittling with her bill a female parakeet accomplishes the widening or shaping the entry hole to the nesting cavity. All these activities contribute to the wear of the bill that is necessary to keep it sharp and functional. Most caged

When a parakeet wants to scratch its head it lifts its leg from behind, between wing and body.

birds have to make do with a whetstone, if that, as a substitute for natural activities. But neither a whetstone nor gnawing on wallpaper, picture frames, or books—about which the bird's keeper is understandably less than enthusiastic—can satisfy a parakeet's need to exercise its bill. Fresh tree branches in the cage or aviary or access to a bird tree are a better substitute and help keep furnishings safe from being nibbled.

Bathing: If a parakeet has a large enough (shallow) bathtub it will first dip its head briefly into the water and then spread its wings in such a way that the entire body gets wet (see color photo on back cover). The bath is followed by a vigorous shake of the feathers and extensive preening. If only a small bath house or a toy tub is provided, the bird will probably be able to wet incompletely only one part of the body at a time. Many pet birds like to take a bath under a dripping faucet, others in a bowl with wet lettuce leaves or in a bunch of wet greens (see page 21). The film by Arendt and Schweiger on the courtship and breeding behavior of Australian parakeets depicts a flock of birds at a watering place. The birds are shown settling down briefly in shallow water, wetting legs and belly, quickly drinking a few sips, and then taking off again. They circle the watering place several times before descending and always stay in the water or next to it for only a few moments. Apparently they do not feel secure enough to take leisurely baths as many caged parakeets do. Instead the wild birds seem nervous and hurried (see color photo on page 110).

Equalizing Temperature

Stretching and raising wings: When it is very hot parakeets often raise and stretch both wings, panting as they do this. This serves the necessary function of keeping the body temperature uniform.

Sometimes the wings are raised but not spread. Probably this behavior has nothing to do with regulating body temperature because it has been observed at a wide range of temperatures. Parakeets also like to stretch the leg and wing of one side simultaneously. Both the raising of the wings and this latter form of stretching are probably equivalents to our stretching after having sat for a long time or after waking up.

Puffing up: When a flock of birds are resting on perches or branches the birds keep at a uniform distance from each other. This spacing is called *individual distance*. If a bird fails to respect this distance and gets too close, the response of the one whose space has been invaded is either to threaten or to move away. But when it is very cold no attention is paid to individual distance. The birds huddle close together with puffed plumage. The reason for this is obvious: Puffing up the feathers and moving close together reduce heat loss. Air is captured in the puffed feathers and acts as an insulating barrier between the body and the outside cold.

Shaking the Feathers

A parakeet shakes its feathers several times in the course of a day. The bird first puffs itself up briefly and then shakes its whole body with a faint rustling sound. The purpose of this gesture may be hygienic, perhaps to shake out dust or dirt or to get all the feathers into place after a bath. But shaking the feathers also seems to provide relief from inner tension, because birds usually go through this motion after out-of-the-ordinary experiences, such as being startled, feeling nervous, having their heads scratched, or rubbing beaks with a partner. Shaking the feathers also serves as a transition from one action to another or from rest to activity.

The Behavior of Parakeets

Yawning

A parakeet yawns by opening its bill slowly, then suddenly opening it wide and shutting it rapidly. People yawn when they are tired or when there is a lack of oxygen in a room. Presumably parakeets yawn for the same reasons. Whether or not this is the case, yawning is just as contagious for parakeets as for humans. If one bird begins to yawn, soon its partner or the whole little flock will follow suit.

Sleeping posture of a parakeet. The bird turns its head backward and tucks it into the back feathers.

Sleeping and Resting

In their Australian homeland parakeets gather in trees to sleep. Caged parakeets, too, retreat at dusk to specific sleeping places in the cage or aviary. In contrast to the wild birds, which sleep in different places every night, most pet birds keep the same sleeping place for years.

Sleeping in a flock affords wild birds protection against predators. If the flock are disturbed they all fly up together and look for another tree to settle down on. If birds in a cage or aviary are disturbed at night this can be hazardous for them because they rise up in such a panic that they sometimes seriously hurt themselves on the grating.

Parakeets are not constantly active during the day; they take rests now and then, and in Australia they have a long siesta in the midday heat. By resting, the wild birds conserve energy during the heat of the day, which is crucial to survival in their harsh environment. The rhythm of sleep and waking hours is no doubt connected to the position of the sun in the sky. Our caged birds, too, adhere to a certain daily rhythm, whether it be dictated by the sun, changes of temperature, or external caretaking routines.

When a parakeet is dozing it sits quietly with closed eyes, slightly puffed feathers, and one leg drawn up into the plumage of the abdomen. The bird assumes the same posture in deep sleep but also turns its head back and tucks its bill into the back feathers (see illustration on left).

Locomotion

The first locomotion you will perhaps observe in a newly purchased bird is its *tripping along a perch*. If the newcomer is not cowering in a corner on the bottom of the cage it is likely to be sitting on a perch and watching its surroundings either shyly or with curiosity. But no wide-awake parakeet can sit still for long, especially if it is excited. So it will start moving back and forth sideways on its perch with tiny, quick steps. Usually its body is at right angles to the perch when it moves like this. Perhaps it will hop to a perch on the opposite side to trip back and forth there, and at some point it will fly to the bottom of the cage or aviary to peck at gravel and food. When moving on the ground in search of food, the parakeet also takes tiny, quick steps, but now the direction is forward rather than sideways. If there is more room than what a cage bottom can provide, the bird will occasionally hop, pushing off from the ground with both feet, and sometimes this *hopping* is combined with a few quick flaps of the wings.

We have already mentioned that parakeets in Australia often cover hundreds of kilometers a day in rapid flight when searching for food and not involved in breeding. It goes without saying that no bird living under human care can ever develop its full flying potential. A pet bird will not be able to develop the stamina necessary for survival in the wild or reach its top flight speeds, no matter how generous the aviary or large the available living room. Nevertheless a healthy bird will take full advantage of an aviary or room for flying and gradually get to know every corner. Usually the parakeet has fixed flight routes around obstacles and favorite landing places. But a parakeet needs at least one companion of its own kind as a stimulus for flying. It is true that a single bird, too, will fly and climb, especially if encouraged by its keeper, but its level of activity does not compare to that of parakeets living in contact with each other. Climbing is just as natural a mode of locomotion for parakeets as flying.

Parakeets like to cover shorter distances by climbing, longer ones by flying. Natural branches in an aviary or climbing trees in a living room quickly become their favorite places since they are good for climbing and for taking off into the air.

If you are keeping one or two parakeets in a cage you will often see them spreading and flapping their wings while hanging on to the perch tightly. They go through the motions of flying without taking to the air. Research done by Kurt Banz shows conclusively that this *beating of the wings* occurs only in birds kept in cages either exclusively or most of the time. Aviary birds do not need this exercise since they have enough opportunity to satisfy their need for flying. The beating of wings is therefore a sign to be heeded by the keeper that the bird is suffering from lack of exercise and is forced by the unnatural confinement of its environment to resort to this unnatural behavior. The situation is different in young birds that have just learned to fly. These birds, too, flap their wings in an aviary or on a climbing tree, even though they have adequate room for flying. They are apparently exercising their joints and flight muscles.

To conclude this section I should like to repeat that birds kept singly move less than pairs or small flocks do. As true flock birds, parakeets respond in mood and activities to the stimulation of fellow birds. If one bird begins to preen itself, its neighbor will soon follow, and broodiness, yawning, and sleepiness are similarly contagious. A bird taking off has the effect of a command; the whole flock is compelled to follow. Let me therefore stress again: Have at least two parakeets if you want to have birds that stay active, keep themselves busy, and remain fit by flying and climbing.

The Behavior of Parakeets

Sensory Capacities

Organisms use their senses to perceive their environment and react to its conditions in a way that is most beneficial to the members of their species. But not all sense organs are equally developed in all creatures. Dogs, for instance, have much better noses than humans and hear sounds that are inaudible to us. About birds in general Konrad Lorenz once said that they were "visual people." But up to now hardly any systematic research has been done on the sensory capacities of parakeets. However, just observing the behavior of parakeets gives us a good indication of which senses are most crucial to dealing with life in the wild.

Like most birds, parakeets *see* very well but differently from us. Some English scientists demonstrated as early as 1931 that birds see the world in colors. This is not surprising. Birds that are active during the day often have conspicuously colored plumage, and the colors can play an active role in social behavior only if they can be seen.

Parakeets—again like many other birds—have a much larger field of vision than humans. Since their eyes are on the sides of the head and register images independently of each other, birds see not only what is going on in front and on the sides but to a considerable extent also what is approaching from behind. This adaptation is important for creatures with little ability to defend themselves. It gives them a constant panoramic view of their surroundings without their having to turn their heads, and it helps them spot a potential enemy and escape. But because its eyes are placed on the sides of the head a parakeet has a considerably smaller range of spatial vision—the area that both eyes take in at once—than humans do. On the other hand, a bird's eye can register up to 150 images per second compared to the human eye's limit of about sixteen. Instantaneous recognition of details is extremely important for fast-flying birds.

Most birds have a very acute sense of *hearing* because calls and songs are a major form of avian communication. Parakeets hear sounds from 400 to probably about 20,000 Hz, although their hearing is best in the range of 1,000 to 3,000 Hz. Within this optimal range parakeets can distinguish minute differences in pitch. The human ear hears sounds from 16 to 20,000 Hz.

Parakeets have a better memory for specific frequencies than we do. This is an important talent because certain calls, especially the shrill alarm cries, have to be sounded spontaneously and accurately if they are to be effective signals. Parakeets are also better than we are at analyzing acoustic signals. What sounds to us like amorphous shrieking is a clearly recognizable sequence of sounds that a bird can reproduce exactly.

Only in the case of a few species, we have some detailed knowledge of how well birds can *smell* and *taste*. As a general rule we assume that these senses are of minor importance to birds. Thus far there have been no conclusive studies about the parakeet's ability to smell and taste. All we have to go on is reports of individual parakeet keepers. Many bird owners let their pets taste human food, completely ignoring the warning that this habit is detrimental to the birds' health. These people like to tell stories of their pets' special preferences that would seem to indicate that parakeets do respond to taste. Perhaps the birds can tell the differences between bitter and salty and sweet and sour. We assume that almost all birds, including parakeets, lack a differentiated sense of smell. We know that many mammals define the borders of their territory by leaving scent marks and that they attract sexual partners with olfactory substances. Birds do neither.

Little is known about the sense of *touch* in parakeets. But it seems almost certain that this sense plays a central role in the female's brooding. With her "brood patches" (see page 89) she can sense both embryonic movements and hatching activity.

One sense that we are barely conscious of but that is of importance to birds is the sense of *vibration*. By means of specialized cells in the legs, the so-called Herbst corpuscles or touch receptors, birds are able to perceive even the most minute vibrations of their perches. This is very important to survival because the ability to sense vibrations gives them warning of impending natural events or of an enemy's approach and serves as a cue for flight. Sensitive as all birds, including parakeets, are to vibrations, they can learn that not all vibrations signal danger. If, for instance, a branch is vibrating because of a light breeze, no bird will fly off. Wind, rain, and storms are familiar natural phenomena. Nevertheless vibration always creates some tension. Parakeets are especially sensitive to vibrations, responding with flight whenever possible. Make sure, therefore, that the permanent location of the cage be absolutely free of vibration. Never put the cage down thoughtlessly on a refrigerator, for instance, even for a few minutes. In its flight reaction the bird might seriously hurt itself.

Useful Addresses

Organizations

American Budgerigar Society
Home office: 141 Hill Street ext.
Naugatuck, CT 06770
Tel.: (203) 729–4810

The Budgerigar Society (England)
57, Stephyn's Chambers, Bank Court
Marlowes, Hemel Hempstead, Herts.
England

The Avicultural Society of Queensland
c/o Mr. Ray Garwood
19 Fahey's Road
Albany Creek, 4035 Qld. Australia

The Golden Triangle Parrot Club
P.O. Box 1574, Station C
Kitchener, Ontario
Canada N2G 4P2

(Young birdkeepers under sixteen may like
to join the Junior Bird League. Full details
can be obtained from J.B.L., c/o *Cage and
Aviary Birds*.)

Bird Magazines

American Cage-Bird Magazine
One Glamore Ct.
Smithtown, NY 11787

The A.F.A. Watchbird
P.O. Box 1125
Garden Grove, CA 92642

Bird Talk
P.O. Box 3940
San Clemente, CA 92672

Cage and Aviary Birds (weekly)
Surrey House
1, Throwley Way
Sutton,
Surrey, SM 1 4QQ
England

Index

Index

Index

Index

between bitter and salty and sweet and sour.
We assume that almost all birds, including
parakeets, lack a differentiated sense of
smell. We know that many mammals define
the borders of their territory by leaving
scent marks and that they attract sexual
partners with olfactory substances. Birds do
neither.

Little is known about the sense of *touch*
in parakeets. But it seems almost certain
that this sense plays a central role in the
female's brooding. With her "brood patches" (see page 89) she can sense both
embryonic movements and hatching activity.

One sense that we are barely conscious of
but that is of importance to birds is the
sense of *vibration*. By means of specialized
cells in the legs, the so-called Herbst corpuscles or touch receptors, birds are able to
perceive even the most minute vibrations of
their perches. This is very important to
survival because the ability to sense vibrations gives them warning of impending natural events or of an enemy's approach and
serves as a cue for flight. Sensitive as all
birds, including parakeets, are to vibrations,
they can learn that not all vibrations signal
danger. If, for instance, a branch is vibrating
because of a light breeze, no bird will fly
off. Wind, rain, and storms are familiar
natural phenomena. Nevertheless vibration
always creates some tension. Parakeets are
especially sensitive to vibrations, responding
with flight whenever possible. Make sure,
therefore, that the permanent location of the
cage be absolutely free of vibration. Never
put the cage down thoughtlessly on a refrigerator, for instance, even for a few minutes. In its flight reaction the bird might
seriously hurt itself.

Useful Addresses

Organizations

American Budgerigar Society
Home office: 141 Hill Street ext.
Naugatuck, CT 06770
Tel.: (203) 729–4810

The Budgerigar Society (England)
57, Stephyn's Chambers, Bank Court
Marlowes, Hemel Hempstead, Herts.
England

The Avicultural Society of Queensland
c/o Mr. Ray Garwood
19 Fahey's Road
Albany Creek, 4035 Qld. Australia

The Golden Triangle Parrot Club
P.O. Box 1574, Station C
Kitchener, Ontario
Canada N2G 4P2

(Young birdkeepers under sixteen may like
to join the Junior Bird League. Full details
can be obtained from J.B.L., c/o *Cage and
Aviary Birds*.)

Bird Magazines

American Cage-Bird Magazine
One Glamore Ct.
Smithtown, NY 11787

The A.F.A. Watchbird
P.O. Box 1125
Garden Grove, CA 92642

Bird Talk
P.O. Box 3940
San Clemente, CA 92672

Cage and Aviary Birds (weekly)
Surrey House
1, Throwley Way
Sutton,
Surrey, SM 1 4QQ
England